2016: *The Cancer in the American Healthcare System*—Helps the reader understand the *real reason* U.S. healthcare is failing.

★★★★★ "Once I started reading this book, I could not put it down."

★★★★★ "If I could give this book ten stars, I would."

★★★★★ "You have got to read this book. It is so informative!"

★★★★★ "How can the information in the book be brought out in the news media and force a change we can live with?

★★★★★ "I felt as though all the missing pieces in my mind were filled in and put together by reading this book."

★★★★★ "I was sucked into this book by the end of the intro!"

★★★★★ "Eye-opening! . . . I think everyone should read this book."

2019: *Curing the Cancer in U.S. Healthcare*—This book takes the reader from reason-for-failure to a simple how-to-fix!

★★★★★ "Every person in the country should read this book . . ."

★★★★★ A Top-50 Amazon reviewer wrote: "the concepts in this well written book offer hope for change!"

★★★★★ "StatesCare is such a simple and obvious solution—when can we move forward on this plan?!?!?"

★★★★★ "I absolutely support . . . change from Obamacare/federally controlled healthcare to StatesCare."

★★★★★ "His arguments are very convincing. . . . I recommend this book to anyone."

Curing the Cancer in U.S. Healthcare

Curing the Cancer in U.S. Healthcare

StatesCare & Market-Based Medicine

Deane Waldman, MD, MBA

ADM Books
Albuquerque, NM

Get Your Free Bonuses

Thank you for buying Curing the Cancer in U.S. Healthcare.
I know you will enjoy it and hope you will share it with others.

You'll find free bonuses available to you at
www.deanewaldman.com.

The bonuses include a downloadable Healthcare Decoder,
videos on healthcare, and articles on important trends and
developments in healthcare.

Additional bonuses will be added periodically such as
new videos, checklists, interviews, bonus chapters,
free e-books, and more.

Thank you for being part of the cure for U.S. healthcare.

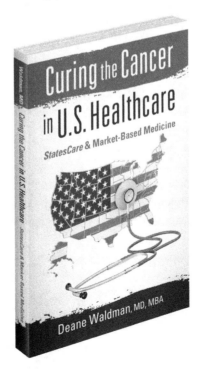

ISBN: 978-0-9847686-9-1

Cover and interior design by Constellation Book Services

A portion of the proceeds from sales of this book will be donated to the Veterans' Initiative of Canine Companions for Independence.

Dedication

This work is dedicated to all my fellow sufferers, those who provide care for patients. Whether it is preventative care to maintain health, medical care for illness, or hospice relief, you get up every day to go work within a system that harasses you, devalues you, and even punishes you for your good deeds. You do this because the welfare of others is your calling.

For those who don't work in healthcare, let me paint you a picture, one with care providers in chains. They do what society wants. They believe, with good reason, that the healthcare system should help them do their noble work and reward them. U.S. healthcare does precisely the opposite.

Your doctor doesn't practice medicine on you, not really. An insurance actuary or government regulator does. He or she tells the doctor what drug you can take, what operation you can have, how long you have to wait before you get the care you need, and whether you will get it, ever! Neither the doctor nor the patient is the medical decision maker.

Every day, virtually every U.S. physician will fight with an insurance bureaucrat to try to get you the care you need. All too often, the doctor will lose . . . and so will you.

Just like doctors, nurses are forced to waste hours each day on administrative tasks and regulatory compliance that do not help patients. Those hours spent in front of a computer screen are hours they can't be with their patients.

The system in which health care providers must function is designed to obstruct, restrain, control, penalize, and punish rather than help medical professionals as they struggle to get you what you need.

This book honors all those who get up every morning knowing they will have to push back against the very system that should encourage, support, and reward them. Health care providers—nurses, doctors, and therapists of all kinds—do this out of dedication to patient welfare. This book is dedicated to them.

Table of Contents

Postscript

Postscript literally means "writing after [first] writing." The postscript here explains why there are two versions of this book.

In 2017, I was the director of the Center for Healthcare Policy at the Texas Public Policy Foundation. In my role, I asked myself what options might be available to Texas if the Lone Star State could free itself from federal control of healthcare. I began work on the possibility of a healthcare system based on free-market principles.

After thinking it through with others at Texas Public Policy Foundation, I modeled the financial details based on data from Texas. I explained this in the book *Curing the Cancer in U.S. Healthcare* and honored the Lone Star State in the subtitle, calling market-based healthcare the "Texas Model."

After the book was released, early readers asked whether market-based healthcare could be used elsewhere than Texas. I had inadvertently implied the market-based approach was limited to Texas. I realized that I had to make sure readers understood that market-based healthcare was potentially useful anywhere. Therefore, I revised the text while leaving the concepts and financial modeling unchanged.

As a result, there were two books titled *Curing the Cancer* in U.S. Healthcare, with different covers and different subtitles. The latest version and only one now available that you are now reading is subtitled, *StatesCare and Market-Based Medicine.*

Introduction

To cure sickness, you need to know the cause, regardless of whether the patient is a sick human or a critically ill system like healthcare. Without knowing the root cause or etiology, you can only palliate the patient's symptoms—you cannot cure him, her, or it.

The main symptoms in *patient* U.S. healthcare are apparent to everyone: too expensive and too little care. Costs are incredible, you can't find a doctor, and when you do find one, you have to wait months to get an appointment.

Healthcare costs are eating our lunch, along with breakfast, dinner, and the mortgage payment! Look at the facts in the table below, starting with the average American family of four, based on a Milliman Medical Index and Income Survey from January 2018.[1] The average family of four spent $28,165—48 percent of all their income, on healthcare costs. The family foregoes more than $13,000 of income in employer support for insurance premium expenses and pays almost half of their take-home pay for out-of-pocket health costs.

Most American families simply cannot afford this. Yet insurance costs keep rising despite the self-styled "Affordable" Care Act of 2010. The nation cannot afford healthcare either. In 1960, the United States expended 5 percent of Gross Domestic Product (GDP) on healthcare. In 2018, U.S. spending on healthcare consumed almost 18 percent of GDP.

Family Budget	Amount	Percentages
Take-home (gross) salary	$58,829	81%
Employer pays for your insurance premiums	$13,430	19%
Potential take-home salary	$72,259	100%
Family Healthcare Costs		
Co-pays and deductibles	$8,685	31%
Insurance premiums (out-of- pocket)	$6,050	21%
Employer-paid premiums	$13,430	48%
Total family annual healthcare costs	$28,165	100%
Healthcare costs as percentage of current take-home pay		48%

"Healthcare" as one word means the system, one that is overspending us into bankruptcy and incurring debt that our children will have to pay back. "Health" . . . "care" as two words is personal service provided by a professional, something that is harder and harder to get, especially in time to save us from illness and death.

Healthcare has been described as a "broken" system. I prefer to view our failing system as a sick person. As such, patient healthcare is in the ICU, on life support.

While we agree how sick healthcare is, people disagree on what to do. Some say we should repeal and replace Obamacare, but sadly, they have no idea what the replacement should be. Some claim that single payer is the answer.[2] People speak with great passion but often have little evidence. Most Americans are simply confused and frustrated. They know both political parties make promises that fail to materialize. Americans know what they don't want and what they have now but are unclear about what they do want.

Curing our failing healthcare system starts with knowing the cause of the illness. I wrote *The Cancer in the American Healthcare System* in order to take readers through the thinking process doctors use when making an etiologic or causative diagnosis. Systems thinkers describe this activity as root cause analysis. In *The Cancer . . .*, we uncovered the reason U.S. healthcare is failing both Americans and the nation: cancer.

Our healthcare system has malignancy located in the federal bureaucracy. It keeps growing and growing, apparently without limit, consuming healthcare funds that are desperately needed to pay for care. The book you hold starts with the diagnosis of cancer and proceeds to cure. It shows how Americans can get the care they need, when and where they need it, at a price they can afford both as individuals and as a nation.

Chapter Notes

1. The 2018 Milliman Medical Index can be found at www.milliman.com/mmi.

2. In a book titled *Single Payer Won't Save Us*, I collected all the evidence and results for single payer systems in Great Britain, Canada, and even our own homegrown single payer disaster, the VA system. The title tells you what I think about single payer. However, you should decide for yourself, based on hard evidence offered there, not emotional rhetoric.

CHAPTER 1

Healthcare Is Critically Ill

You are a doctor. A patient walks into your office complaining of headaches. You introduce yourself and sit down in front of your computer. You find a pain killer that is authorized by the patient's health plan in its pharmacy benefits management program. You then print the prescription, using only a government-approved printer, of course. You hand the top copy of the triplicate form to the patient. The receptionist gives the patient a bill for services rendered and ushers him out the door. You have successfully *cared for* the patient within your allotted 15-minute time benchmark and will get high marks on your efficiency scorecard.

No history taken. No physical exam performed. No lab tests or imaging of any kind—MRI, X-ray, echo, or CT scan. No review of patient's medical records or reading of previous medical literature on other patients with similar complaints. No differential diagnosis. No attempt to find the cause of the patient's symptoms. Just a painkiller and out the door. Was this good medical practice? If you were this patient, would you be satisfied? Of course not!

That is precisely how Congress has *treated* a "patient" named U.S. Healthcare System for more than five decades. Federal solutions invariably unfold the same way. They announce a crisis in healthcare, write new regulations, and thus spend more money on the federal bureaucracy, leaving fewer and fewer dollars to spend on care that patients need.

No wonder patient Healthcare is now critically ill in the ICU on life support. Absent a miracle, patient Healthcare is going to die. When that happens, Americans will no longer be able to get the lifesaving they need. And then, as some politicians have predicted, we will see people "dying needlessly in the streets."

Washington's fixes-that-fail-or-backfire

Medicare was created as part of the Social Security Act of 1965. It was supposed to be a giant national savings account that would provide for our medical needs after retirement. The Congressional Budget Office (CBO) assured Congress the program would cost $12 billion. In fact, 25 years after its passage, a financial audit of the Medicare program found that Congress underestimated the expense by an astonishing 854 percent! Instead of $12 billion, Medicare cost more than $100 billion.

The CBO now predicts the Medicare Trust Fund will be insolvent by 2026.[1] This means Medicare will be unable to pay for senior medical needs like drugs, nursing care, or operations. Those who contributed for 40 years of work life and were promised medical security in retirement will be left out in the cold. Grandma will fall off the ledge because Medicare won't be able to pay for her walker, much less a wheelchair.

The year 1965 saw the creation of not only Medicare, but Medicaid as well, both parts of President Lyndon Johnson's Great Society. Medicaid was jointly funded by both the states and the federal government. The law provided for 51 distinctly different programs, each one administered by the individual state or the District of Columbia. Section 1801 in the 1965 Medicaid law confirmed that the states were supposed to be in charge of their own programs. The title was "Prohibition Against Any Federal Interference."[2]

Slowly, piece by piece, rule by rule, Washington took over administration of every aspect of state Medicaid programs, implementing a federal, centralized, one-size-fits-all approach.[3] When I write "every aspect of state Medicaid programs," that is not hyperbole. When New Mexico was creating its Health Insurance Exchange, the Washington-based Centers for Medicare and Medicaid Services (CMS) even dictated the font (typeface) and type size of the eligibility forms that patients must complete.

One size does not fit all. It doesn't even fit most! Any single healthcare mandate does not apply equally to all Americans, in our diverse regions, with a wide variety of medical needs and different resources.

Medicaid has grown to be the largest single line item in most state budgets. Yet the states do not control how that money, *their* money, is spent—Washington does. As a result of Washington's takeover of administrative control over state Medicaid programs, these programs are failing enrollees, the states, and our nation.

Entitlement reform is a favorite sound bite for both parties. Both Democrats and Republicans claim their party's latest fix will solve the Medicaid entitlement problem, yet they never really "fix" anything. The solution is always the same: more government, more regulations, more spending, and blaming the previous administration for the ever-growing, all-consuming entitlement monster.

Systems theory[4] is the study of how systems such as organizations, institutions, and even government agencies function, particularly when they are failing. This discipline has a term that describes both Medicare and Medicaid: fixes-that-failed-or-backfired. This means there is a problem with the program, that a solution was implemented to fix the problem, and that the problem was not fixed or actually got worse.

Washington's fixes for Medicare "backfired" so badly that, in less than ten years, Medicare will leave seniors without medical care. Medicare will run out of money. The expansion of Medicaid pursuant to implementing Obamacare caused state programs to reduce payments to providers, which cut the availability of care for the people who need it most.

In the early twentieth century, people who needed medical care but could not pay for it received their care either through private charities or in county-supported hospitals.[5] With the collapse of the county hospital system in the 1960s, sick indigent persons and poor pregnant women began showing up in large numbers in hospital emergency rooms. Hospitals started playing a game of hot potato. They *dumped* critically ill, nonpaying patients to other hospitals.

In the 1980s, newspapers started headlining tragedies like "Mother

Dies Giving Birth in Alley" and "If You're Sick and Poor, Too Bad." Without any hard evidence, Congress passed EMTALA (Emergency Medical Transport and Labor Act of 1985), also known as the "anti-dumping" law. EMTALA mandated that any hospital accepting federal funds, that is, almost all U.S. hospitals that had emergency rooms, were required to "provide for an appropriate medical screening examination . . . [and] such treatment as may be required to stabilize the medical condition," whether the patient had insurance or not.[6] An uninsured person having a heart attack could enter the ER, be sent to the ICU, and receive all necessary care, including open heart surgery, without having any payment source to cover the hospital bill.

EMTALA created a huge federally mandated financial loss for hospitals. "Huge" is no exaggeration. The average profit margin for most large urban hospitals is roughly two percent. The cost of uncompensated care is typically at least 20 percent of a hospital's operating budget.[7] Hospitals were forced to adopt creative accounting tricks and shady billing practices; otherwise they had to close their doors. By solving one problem—care for the uninsured—EMTALA created another one: the unfunded mandate.

The CEO of a well-known insurance company had a hernia repair at a famous hospital. (The CEO's name is withheld for his own protection.) At discharge, he was handed a bill for $28,440.28. Believing the cost was exorbitant, the insurance CEO went to talk with the hospital's chief financial officer (CFO). Line by line, item by item, service by service, they went through the five-page bill. Each time, the CEO demurred, saying the charge was too high. Finally, the CFO threw up his hands exclaiming, "Blame EMTALA, not me. The excessive charges on your bill are needed to pay for the care of people who have no insurance."

The Health Insurance Portability and Accountability Act of 1996 (HIPAA) was another example of a Washington fix-that-fails-or-backfires. In the mid-1990s, many people were losing their jobs. Most workers had employer-supported health insurance through their jobs. As companies had to reduce their operating costs, they used "reductions in force," or "RIFs," a nicer way of saying the company was getting rid of their employees. When people lost jobs, families lost employer-sup-ported health insurance coverage. Congress said HIPAA would make health insurance portable across the job market.

HIPAA failed to make insurance portable, certainly not in an afford-able way. It did expand Medicaid eligibility, but how is that related to portability? By tightening the security protocols for sharing medical in-formation, HIPAA made communication between care providers *much* more difficult. As a result, the likelihood of medical errors *increased!*[8] HIPAA joins the group of Washington's fixes-that-fail-or- backfire.

Congress's most recent "fix" for our sick healthcare system is the Affordable Care Act (ACA). When you strip away all the political hy-perbole and disinformation, the ACA has been proven to produce the following results:

- Insurance has become more expensive, not less expensive.

- Access to care has gone down—care has become less available.

- Washington has spent an additional $1.8 trillion, bending the cost curve upward![9] (The GDP of Canada is $1.8 trillion.)

- Many patients cannot keep the doctor they like, in contrast to what was promised.

- Maneuvering through the ACA website and structure to access government-approved insurance plans is nothing short of torture. See figure 1-1.[10]

- If an ACA insurance plan is chosen, the forms (i.e., 1095-A, 8962) and tax ramifications for subsidies are additional nightmares for patients.

Representative Kevin Brady of Texas instructed his staff to create an organizational chart of the ACA. This task took them four months. The result is shown in figure 1-1. The organizational structure defies understanding and gives new meaning to the phrase complex organization. I challenge you to identify who is in charge of what and who reports to whom. Most important, how does this structure improve patient care?

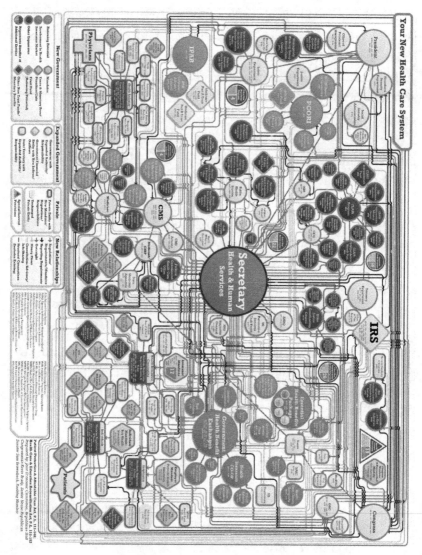

Figure 1-1: ACA Organizational Chart

Washington's behavior is clear and repetitive. They identify a problem, call it a crisis, and use the so-called "impending disaster" as a lever to expand government administrative control and regulatory authority. Then they allocate even more money to bureaucracy, taking it away from patient care.

Figure 1-2: Spending on Bureaucracy Reduces Care

A huge truck pulls up carrying all the money we are going to spend this year on healthcare. The rear ramp comes down and bags of money start rolling out (figure 1-2). Washington's administration, regulation, and compliance oversight, symbolized by the man with the Congress-shaped hat, takes the biggest number of cash bags. Next to him stands the Monopoly Man who represents the corporate practice of medicine, including insurance, hospitals, and big Pharma. He takes another large pile of money. The small number of dollars remaining will float down the ramp and become available to pay for patient care.

Washington diverts trillions of "healthcare" dollars to itself, thus denying Americans desperately needed care.

Proof

There is a mountain of evidence confirming bad medical outcomes in patients with government-supplied insurance, largely due to inadequate access to care. The fiscal impacts are equally negative, for both the individual and our country.

Is Our Care Sufficient to Our Needs?

A February 2017 national survey[11] reported that the maximum wait time to see a family physician in mid-sized U.S. cities had risen to 122 days. That is four months to find out if the pain in your belly is gas, an ulcer, or cancer.

An internal audit[12] of the Veterans Affairs (VA) health system concluded, "47,000 veterans may have died waiting for approval for medical care." Our military veterans experienced "death-by-queueing" just as Britons do in their vaunted NHS (National Health Service), as well as our neighbors to the north in Canada.[13]

Death-by-queueing refers to a person dying from a treatable illness while waiting for care that could have saved his life if it were provided in time. For example, burn victims are more likely to survive if cared for in specialized burn units rather than in a general hospital environment. Canada has allocated an amount of money for a number of burn units that is insufficient for the number of burn victims. There is a long waiting list to get in. People die waiting in line when they might be saved if they could be admitted to a burn unit.

There are numerous reports of government-insured Americans dying because they couldn't get needed care in time. Deamonte Driver was a 12-year-old Maryland boy who died from complications of a cavity in his tooth.[14] He couldn't get dental care because the Medicaid dental reimbursement schedules were so low, there were no pediatric dentists willing to accept Medicaid patients.

After Illinois expanded Medicaid under the Affordable Care Act, access to care was so delayed that 752 residents died waiting in line for care.

In a national survey after surgery, Medicaid recipients did no better than the uninsured, and thus billions of taxpayer dollars were wasted.[15] A study of Hepatitis C patients showed that Medicaid-insured patients often could not get the life-saving drugs they needed and, as a result, they died.[16]

If you compare the process for medical care in the United States with those of single payer nations, we do better in some areas and worse in others.

Table 1-1: Comparison of U.S. Healthcare versus Single Payer Systems

Surrogate Metric of Quality	U.S.	Single Payer Systems		
		U.K.	Canada	Sweden
Get timely care reminders	#3	#5	#9	#10
Reg. MD coordinates care	#3	#1	#4	#8
Reg. MD gives clear & complete instructions	#5*	#1	#5*	#11
Delays in notification	#9	#2	#11	#8
Reg. MD does not have sufficient information	#10	#7	#6	#11
Hospital follow-up care	#1	#2	#4	#8
Post-hospital communication with reg. MD	#3	#7*	#9	#7*
Overall timeliness of care	#5	#3	#11	#1
Wait ≥4 months for non emergency surgery	#6	#4	#9	#5

U.S.=United States. U.K.=United Kingdom. Ranking (#) is from study of 11 industrialized nations; #1 is best and #11 is worst. Reg. MD=primary doctor. (*)=tied for position. GDP=-gross domestic product.

Source: Davis, Schoen, and Stremikis, "Mirror, Mirror on the Wall: How the Performance of the U.S. Health Care System Compares Internationally, 2010 Update."

Some people use national longevity statistics as an indicator of success for a healthcare system. This is unwise. How long a large population lives is much more related to culture, diet, exercise, lifestyle, and genetics than to anything that doctors and nurses do for individual patients.

Fiscal Consequences

Though most commentators discuss only cost, and short-term cost at that, the measure we all should be using is *value*: benefits received for money expended. Based on the value metric, the United States does poorly when compared to other countries. We receive an average amount of benefit, and yet we spend double what most nations spend. Because we do not get double the benefits, the United States is not getting proper value for healthcare dollars expended.

When we look solely at cost, what was individually unaffordable before Obamacare is now even *more* unaffordable. (The editors said that "more unaffordable" is improper grammar. I left it that way because "more unaffordable" communicates quite clearly the reality we all face.) Until the real estate collapse of 2008–2009, medical bills constituted the #1 reason for filing personal bankruptcy in the United States. Now, costs related to healthcare average 48 percent of a family's budget and are the biggest expense in the average family budget (See table in the introduction.)

The national fiscal picture is equally grim. In 1970, the United States was spending roughly the same amount per capita on healthcare as other developed nations. By 2010, we were spending more than double. Then, in 2010, we spent an additional $2 trillion for the ACA. How did that make healthcare "more affordable"?

We can also compare healthcare spending with a country's GDP. The higher the GDP, the richer a nation is. Figure 1-3 shows that most countries fall on a similar cost line, but there are two outliers, countries quite different from most others.

Luxembourg is first, where people are very wealthy and spend only a moderate amount of their wealth on healthcare.

Then, there is the United States, where individuals are moderately wealthy but spend much, much more on healthcare than anyone else.

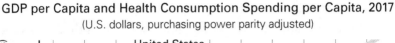

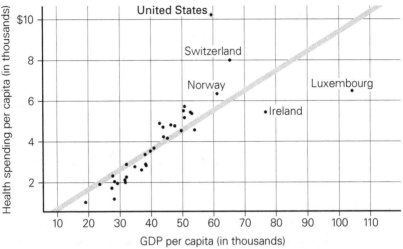

Figure 1-3: Healthcare Spending: U.S. and Other Nations

The consequences of overspending on healthcare are worse for the states than for the federal government for one obvious reason. The Treasury Department can print money—the states cannot. So, for example, Texas may create budget allocations for 2018–2019, but Washington tells the Lone Star State how it is required by law to spend the first 30 percent of its budget, on Medicaid.

The situation is even more grave (pun intended) for states, like New Mexico, that expanded Medicaid under the ACA. Despite $3 billion shiny new federal dollars in Land of Enchantment coffers, mandated costs of Medicaid were $3.4 billion. Thus, New Mexico Medicaid had a budget shortfall in 2017 of $417 million. To balance its budget, the state had to cut medical reimbursements to providers. Medicaid expansion gave more people insurance and left them with fewer service providers.

Senator Everett Dirksen is famous for an offhand remark: "A billion here, a billion there, and pretty soon you're talking real money!"[17] We are all aware that the United States is spending too much "real money" on healthcare. Where is it all going?

Are the insurance companies getting rich with their rent-seeking behaviors? There is some truth to that allegation. Others say the doctors and hospitals are the ones ripping us off. However, that is less true. The public thinks providers get paid what is written on the bill for services rendered, while in fact, providers are paid a fraction, often a very small fraction, of the price listed on the bill.

One way to answer the question of "Where does all the money go?" is to calculate dollar efficiency.[18] This measures the difference between money that goes into making something and the value a customer or end-user receives. For an auto manufacturer, dollar efficiency is the ratio of the cost to make the vehicle compared to the value that consumers perceive when buying the car.

In healthcare, dollar efficiency would be the amount of money spent compared to the quantity and quality of care patients receive. For simplicity, we can use "care received" as an indicator of quality and quantity. Thus, dollar efficiency in healthcare could be calculated as the amount of money we put into healthcare compared to how much care we get.

When you do that calculation, the minimum numbers for dollar efficiency are 60–69 percent meaning 31–40 percent of healthcare spending provides no care for patients.[19] Those estimates were made before Obamacare added nearly $2 trillion of additional bureaucratic expense. When you include cost of the ACA, dollar inefficiency in healthcare approaches 50 percent. In simple terms, close to half of all our "healthcare" spending produces no care.

The answer to "Where does all that money go?" is to healthcare bureaucracy, administration, rules, regulations, and compliance. The money goes to the system rather than the service. For a sense of perspective, we are wasting almost as much on healthcare bureaucracy as the entire country of Canada will produce in 2018: $1.79 trillion.

There are other, lesser-in-dollar-volume reasons for wasteful spending. Hundreds of millions of dollars are consumed by fraud and abuse as well as honest error. The regulations are impossibly complex, constantly changing, and often contradictory so that sometimes, it is simply impossible to comply with all the rules. The cost of defensive medicine has been estimated to be as high as $46 billion a year.[20]

Before we conclude this first chapter, let's lighten the mood with a funny but real-world story. A woman brought a very limp duck to a veterinary surgeon. As she laid her pet on the table, the vet pulled out his stethoscope and listened to the bird's chest. After a moment or two, the vet shook his head sadly and said, "I'm sorry, your duck, Cuddles, has passed away." The distressed woman wailed, "Are you sure?"

"Yes, I am sure. The duck is dead," replied the vet. "How can you be so sure?" she protested. "I mean you haven't done any testing on him or anything. He might just be in a deep sleep or something." The vet rolled his eyes, turned around, and left the room.

He returned a few minutes later with a black Labrador retriever. As the duck's owner looked on in amazement, the dog stood on his hind legs, put his front paws on the examination table, and sniffed the duck from top to bottom. He then looked up at the vet with sad eyes and shook his head from side to side. The vet patted the dog on the head and took it out of the room.

A few minutes later, he returned with a feline. The cat jumped on the table and also delicately sniffed the bird from head to tail. The cat sat back on its haunches, turned to the vet, shook its head, meowed softly, and strolled out of the room. The vet went to his computer, hit a few keys, and produced a bill, which he handed to the woman. The duck's owner took the bill and read it.

"$250?!" she cried, "Just to tell me my duck is dead?" The vet shrugged, "I'm sorry. If you had just taken my word for it, the bill would have been $20, but with the Lab report and the cat scan, it's now $250."

Conclusion

The U.S. healthcare system is clearly failing the American people. We can't get the care we need in time to save us from illness or even death! We are spending more than we can afford and piling debt onto future generations.

As the late-night advertising heads shout from our TV sets, "But wait, there's more!!" Isn't health care a right? And if it is, shouldn't everyone automatically get it, and for free? Let's explore this in the next chapter.

Chapter Notes

1. The "2013 Annual Report of the Boards of Trustees of the Federal Hospital Insurance and Federal Supplementary Medical Insurance Trust Funds" predicted that Medicare would be insolvent by 2030. A 2018 report revised that estimate to 2026. At that time, Medicare will be unable to provide care that seniors need. Note that even now, Medicare does not cover the most predictable and often necessary senior medical need: long-term nursing care.

2. The precise wording of Section 1801 of the 1965 Medicaid law is as follows: "Nothing in this title shall be construed to authorize any Federal officer or employee to exercise any supervision or control over the practice of medicine or the manner in which medical services are provided, or over the selection, tenure, or compensation of any officer or employee of any institution, agency, or person providing health services; or to exercise any supervision or control over the administration or operation of any such institution, agency, or person" See Public Law 89–97, Hospital Insurance Program, 1965, page 291.

3. Mary Katherine Stout's 2006 paper "Medicaid: Yesterday, Today, and Tomorrow: A Short History of Medicaid Policy and Its Impact on Texas" gives a vivid portrayal of the gradual, subtle, and incremental takeover of state Medicaid programs by the federal government, by giving the states their own tax revenue back. The states could have prevented this by simply "resisting federal blandishments," as suggested by Chief Justice Roberts in NFIB (*National Federation of Independent Business*) *v. Sebelius* in 2012. See the Healthcare Decoder in this book for more on the case.

4. Systems theory begins with the premise that a system, whether that *system* is a human body, a corporation, or an entire industry like healthcare, succeeds or fails through the interaction of the parts of the system. No matter how good your heart is, you won't survive if your heart does not interact well with your kidneys, liver, and lungs. When there is a problem with one part of a system, fixing it without including the fix's effects on other parts often makes things worse, not better. Saving money in *Medicare* can make people sicker in *Medicaid*. Such a result is what systems thinkers call a fix-that-fails-or-backfires. This descriptor applies painfully well to what Congress has done repeatedly over the years to healthcare.

5. Marvin Olasky's book *The Tragedy of American Compassion* tells the compelling story of charitable activities in the United States. It is sad to note that

most of the lessons learned through that experience seem to have been lost in the current ascendancy of progressivism. At its height in the late 1950s, Cook County Hospital had more than 3,000 beds, served hundreds of thousands of indigent or impoverished residents of Chicago, and was one of the most sought-after training programs in the country.

6.   The exact wording can be found in "Examination and treatment for emergency medical conditions and women in labor," Social Security Laws, Sec. 1867 [42 U.S.C. 1395dd].

7.   In 2003, I analyzed the cost of uncompensated care for a major university hospital. Though the report was never published, it was made available at a meeting open to the public. The annual operating budget was $960 million and the cost of uncompensated care was $235 million (24 percent).

8.   See "Privacy or Safety?" published by the Agency for Healthcare Research and Quality, July/August 2015.

9.   The initial government estimate for the cost of Obamacare was $900 billion over ten years. It was later revised to $1.1 trillion, then $1.6 trillion, and eventually $2.6 trillion. The latest estimate is $1.76 trillion. Such wide variability of estimates indicates the limitations in Washington's ability to accurately predict true costs.

10. The designers of the ACA knew the law was incomprehensibly complex. So they built into the law a requirement for states to hire "navigators" to help patients find their way around through the maze of federal regulations, exceptions, exemptions, and legal language.

11. Merritt Hawkins is a national market research company that performed a survey in January and February 2017 titled "2017 Survey of Physician Appointment Wait Times."

12. The Veterans Health Administration's 2015 report was titled "Review of Alleged Mismanagement at the Health Eligibility Center."

13. Read what you need to know, which is more than you *want* to know, about death-by-queueing in my book *The Cancer in the American Healthcare System* (2015).

14. The tragic death of Deamonte Driver was front-page news for weeks. Nick Horton originally reported the Illinois deaths online, but this too became a national print media sensation.

15. The study by Dr. Damien LaPar et al., "Primary Payer Status Affects Mortality for Major Surgical Operations," includes details of post-surgical results and death rates. The authors concluded, "Medicaid payer status was associated with the longest length of stay . . . highest total costs ($P < 0.001$)" and an in-hospital mortality similar to those who were uninsured.

16. The chief of medicine at Inova Fairfax Hospital, Dr. Zobair Younossi, reported the findings on June 3, 2018, at a meeting of *Digestive Disease Week*.

17. According to Factchecker, no one could find proof that the late, great Senator from Illinois ever uttered those words.

18. Years ago, I tried to write a song titled "Where Has All the Money Gone?" using the 1950s Pete Seeger melody from "Where Have All the Flowers Gone?" I quickly learned how hard it is to be a lyricist.

19. In 2003, 11 years before the ACA bureaucratic costs had to be paid, Harvard researchers (Woolhandler et al., *New England Journal of Medicine*, 349:8) reported that bureaucracy consumed 31 percent of U.S. healthcare spending. In *The Cancer in the American Healthcare System* (2015), we reported that at least 40 percent was wasteful spending on bureaucracy. The ACA has certainly increased spending on bureaucracy.

20. "National Costs of the Medical Liability System" by Mello et al. in *Health Affairs*. Most scientific articles are written to expose objective truth. Unfortunately, some are designed in advance to prove a point. Many cost analyses in healthcare, from both government and the academic community, fall into the latter category. I do not know if Mello's article is fact or spun data, but it was the best I could find. Consider it possible, even likely, while maintaining a small amount of skepticism as well.

CHAPTER 2

Health Care *Cannot* Be a Right

What is healthcare? The answer depends on how it is spelled. As one word, *healthcare* refers to a complex industrial system that consumes close to 20 percent of U.S. gross domestic product (GDP). When *health care* is two words, it describes a legally protected, intimate, fiduciary relationship between a patient and physician. Health care is the work product of a professional that is purchased by a consumer, also known as a patient.

What is a right? The dictionary says a right is "a moral or legal entitlement to have or obtain something or to act in a certain way." A right is an entitlement. You don't have to qualify for what you are entitled to. You don't have to pay for a right.

The First Amendment to the Constitution gives all Americans the right to free speech. No one needs to qualify. There is no test to pass or forms to fill out. There is no cost to speak your mind. Exercising a fundamental right is not a commercial activity.[1]

The founding document of the United States of America is the Declaration of Independence. It is much more than simply a declaration of war. It defined in clear and ringing terms that Americans' singular, highest, and most basic right is freedom.

Health care, as two words, cannot be a right, not in a country where the overarching right of all the people is freedom.

- Health care is a personal service that one person provides to another in exchange for money.

- If a person has a right to a provider's care, then the patient doesn't have to pay for that care.

- If a patient has a right to the personal service of a provider, then the provider is denied his or her freedom.

- If patients have a "right" to a provider's personal service—when, where, and whatever the patient wants—with no requirement for payment, that turns providers into slaves.

Federal Healthcare Is Unconstitutional

Based on the Constitution, there are several reasons why healthcare should not be controlled by the federal government. First, the Founding Fathers did not simply *forget* about health care: five of the signatories to the Declaration of Independence were physicians. Many more of the delegates to the Constitutional Convention were doctors.

Second, the Tenth Amendment clarifies the relationship between the federal government and the states. "The powers not delegated to the United States [meaning the federal government] by the Constitution, nor prohibited by it to the states, are reserved to the states respectively, or to the people." Thus, the federal government has authority only in the areas specified to it in the Constitution, such as "common defense," interstate commerce, and making our borders secure. Healthcare was never "delegated" to Washington. Therefore, healthcare is reserved "to the states respectively, or to the people."

The Commerce Clause in the Constitution was used as precedent to defend the ACA when challenged at the Supreme Court in 2012.[2] Yet nearly two hundred years earlier, the fourth Chief Justice of the U.S. Supreme Court, John Marshall, one of the staunchest upholders of the

Constitution, wrote that "health laws of every description" are reserved exclusively to the states and not the federal government.[3]

It can't be much clearer than that. The people in their states, not the federal government, should decide healthcare.

There is a fourth, practical reason why federal control of healthcare is unconstitutional. A federal obligation to provide health care would require Washington to deny caregivers their freedom. How else would patients get care? What if no one wanted to go to medical or nursing schools? What if doctors refused to work for menial salaries? What happens when, as now, doctors are forced to do what Washington tells them to do instead of what they believe is in their individual patients' best interests?

Conclusion

Health care cannot be a right, not in the U.S.A. Not in a nation founded on one over-arching right: freedom. Not in a country steeped in rule of law, where slavery was legally banned 156 years ago.

Chapter Notes

1. If you reread the Bill of Rights, the first ten Amendments to the U.S. Constitution, our Founding Fathers' intent is clear. All ten Amendments are protection of individual freedom from the concentration of power that is called the federal government. The First Amendment says the government can't stop you from speaking your mind or praying however you wish, or not praying at all. The Third and Fourth Amendments say that you control your home and person, not the government. The Fifth through Eighth Amendments give you legal protections against a tyrannical government. And the Tenth Amendment very clearly limits the powers of the central authority, saying healthcare "is reserved to the states, not Washington."

2. The 2012 Supreme Court Case was *NFIB (National Federation of Independent Business) v. Sebelius*, who at that time was Secretary of Health and Human Services. The Court ruled that the ACA's Individual Mandate was unconstitutional, but it could be preserved if it were reconstituted as a tax. Two interesting notes: (1) In the NFIB case, the Obama administration argued that the individual mandate could not be severed from the rest of the law, as the whole structure of the law depended on it. The 2017 Tax Reform and Jobs Act set the

Obamacare individual "tax" at zero, meaning it generated no revenue and, thus, effectively ceased to exist. A lawsuit was filed in 2018 claiming that because the Obamacare regulations cannot be separated from the tax and the tax is null and void, then the whole law should be declared null and void. It may be years before this case reaches the Supreme Court; (2) In 2012, Chief Justice Roberts wrote that the states had a straightforward way to ignore federal healthcare mandates: they simply should "resist federal blandishments," meaning if they don't take federal money, they don't have to comply with federal rules.

3. John Marshall was Chief Justice of the U.S. Supreme Court from 1801 to 1835. He is considered one of the most influential legal thinkers in our nation's history. Writing about the use of the Commerce Clause in *Gibbons v. Ogden* (1824), Marshall said that the federal government has no business promulgating any health laws, none at all, period.

CHAPTER 3

Healthcare Has Cancer

In the early part of the twentieth century, two events occurred that drove the cost of both health care, the service, and healthcare, the system, into the stratosphere. First, there were remarkable advances in medical technology. Doctors could treat conditions that were previously beyond their reach.

Cures became possible for infection, heart failure, and even cancer, but they were very expensive. Second, the rise of government-controlled healthcare and the development of the third-party payment structure eliminated the two free-market forces that keep prices down: buyers' incentive to economize and competition among sellers.

The great management guru Russell Ackoff taught us there are four ways to fix a problem, whether it is a small matter or something as huge as our sick healthcare system.[1] You can absolve, solve, resolve, or dissolve a problem.

- *Absolve* means that you change nothing: you just forgive and forget.
- When *solving* a problem, you make things better than they currently are.
- *Resolving* a problem refers to making outcomes the best they can be *under the given circumstances*. Many people confuse this

with a cure. However, resolving leaves the root cause in place. The problem can recur.

- To *dissolve* a problem, you find the root cause and eliminate it. When the root cause is gone, all the symptoms—the bad results or outcomes—disappear and can never return.

When you resolve an issue, the problem can come back later or a new, related problem can appear. Dissolving is the best way to handle any difficulty. When the root cause ceases to exist, the symptoms cannot return. Treatment of diabetes can demonstrate the distinctions between solve, resolve, and dissolve.

Diabetes is a problem with the regulation of glucose (sugar) in the body. Insulin is a molecule made in the pancreas that regulates how much glucose stays in the blood versus how much goes from the blood into the cells. When you have diabetes, you don't produce enough insulin or the insulin you do produce doesn't work right.

There are two harmful consequences of diabetes. The excess sugar in the blood makes you dehydrated and disturbs the balance of electrolytes in your blood. The lack of sugar inside the cells prevents organs like the liver, kidney, and heart from working properly. Acid builds up in the blood. If balance is not restored, you may die.

If you *solve* diabetes, you replace the lost water and electrolytes, counteract the excess acid in the blood, and force the heart to work harder. If you *resolve* diabetes, you restore the proper amount of insulin in the blood. Resolving is the best we can do today. Medical science cannot (yet) dissolve, or cure, diabetes.

To *dissolve* diabetes, first you must know the root cause, or etiology. We do, sort of. There are specialized cells inside the pancreas that control the production of insulin. In diabetes, these cells do not work properly. That is the first half of the root cause, but the second half is unknown. Doctors do not know why these cells cease to function normally. When doctors learn what causes the pancreas cells to fail, they can help them return to good function. That will dissolve the root cause, and thus will cure diabetes.

Curing (dissolving) diabetes is another medical miracle that is likely to occur in the next fifty years. I can absolutely guarantee it will be expensive. Most things of great value are.

Diagnosing Patient Healthcare

The symptoms of healthcare system failure are obvious: national overspending, unaffordable care as well as unaffordable insurance, and inadequate access to care. What is the root cause, or what doctors call the etiologic diagnosis? We can find the answer by using a favorite mantra of forensic accountants: follow the money. In 2017, the United States spent $3.5 trillion on healthcare. At least 40 percent, more than $1 trillion, was paid to support and expand federal bureaucracy, administration, rules, regulations, and compliance. The term that describes this phenomenon is *bureaucratic diversion*.[2] The result is too little money left to pay for care after paying the bureaucracy first.

Between 1970 and 2010, the number of health care providers increased more than 100 percent, the dark grey area in figure 3-1. Over the same 40 years, the number of healthcare bureaucrats (light grey area) grew by more than 3,000 percent. The data only goes as far as 2010: it does not include the further growth of bureaucracy induced by the Affordable Care Act.

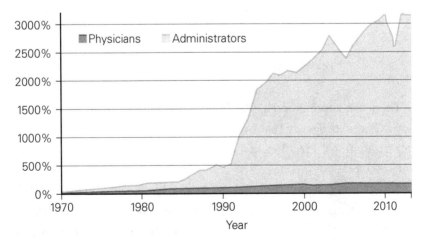

Figure 3-1: Growth in Supply of Doctors and Bureaucrats

Before asking yourself whether healthcare really *needs* that number of bureaucrats, consider the expense. In 2017, there were 953,000 licensed physicians in the United States. The number of healthcare actuaries, accountants, administrators, agents, billers and coders, compliance officers, consultants, in-person assisters, lawyers, managers, navigators, regulators, reviewers, and rule writers in healthcare is not known but certainly is more than ten million. Furthermore, federal employees are more highly compensated, salary plus benefits, than those who do the same job in the private sector as in figure 3-2.

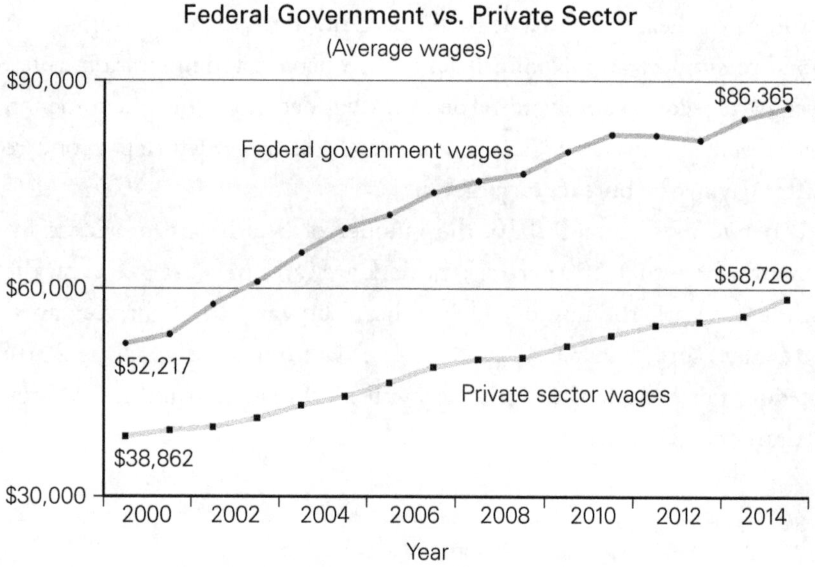

Federal Government vs. Private Sector
(Average wages)

Figure 3-2: Average Wages: Federal and Private Sector

There are approximately 50,000 licensed physicians in the state of Texas. The state agency that oversees their compliance with federal and state regulations, Health and Human Services Commission, employs more than 60,000 bureaucrats.

To paraphrase John Dunne's moving sermon from the mid-17th century that was immortalized by Ernest Hemingway's book *For Whom the Bell Tolls*, "Never send to know to whom the money goes, it goes to ...them."[3]

Taxpayers pay the costs for healthcare bureaucrats twice. First, taxpayers pay financially: bureaucrat salaries, benefits, pensions, overhead and other indirect costs. But, second and more important, taxpayers pay *medically* by reduced access to care. There are only limited numbers of health care providers. Money paid to bureaucrats is money that cannot be spent on providers—bureaucratic diversion. It is not simply fiscal cost of bureaucracy that hamstrings healthcare. In many ways the secondary "costs" of government are more harmful, especially long-term and particularly in the pharmaceutical world, where the 800-pound gorilla is the FDA.

In 1962, Congress passed the Kefauver-Harris Amendments to the Food and Drug Act of 1938. While their intention was to secure a safe, reliable, effective supply of pharmaceutical agents, they turned the Federal Drug Agency into a Greek god: capricious, willful, often harming their "subjects" knowingly, and with essentially limitless power.[4] Watch how the federal bureaucracy put another nail in the coffin of new antibiotics.

The FDA has regulatory controls for every aspect of the pharmaceutical industry, including planning, research, development, testing, manufacturing, even the packaging, and especially the marketing. Their arduous and costly process has put a huge damper on the creation of new drugs, especially antibiotics. Between 1983 and 1987, the FDA approved 16 new antibiotics. From 2003 to 2007, despite the development of antibiotic-resistant organisms, the FDA approved only five, and since then, none. Here's why.

Recall 2001, when two senators and several media offices were exposed to anthrax through the mail. Cipro (ciproflaxin) is an antibiotic primarily used for urinary tract infections, but it also kills anthrax. Bayer, the German pharmaceutical giant, was charging $2.00 a pill. The U.S. federal government wanted to stockpile 100 million pills, just in case. Congress did not want to pay $200 million for a "just in case," and so they browbeat the manufacturer to lower the price to $0.95 a pill.

At that time, Cipro was supposedly under patent protection. Bayer and every pharmaceutical manufacturer learned a bitter lesson: patent protection is meaningless when the federal government wants something. As a consequence, pharmaceutical manufacturers will be increasingly reluctant to develop new antibiotics and other drugs, for that matter. If patents don't protect, how can pharmaceutical manufacturers ever recover the massive costs that the FDA imposes, on top of the billions pharmaceutical companies expend in research and development.

To save $100 million, which is 0.005 percent of the cost of the ACA, we have prevented the next round of "wonder drugs."[5] When the federal bureaucracy doesn't want to play by the rules, they just change them!

The Cipro story is just one of a host of examples of what happens when the federal government dominates the healthcare "market" and dictates prices: you get less of the service or product. Keep that in mind when someone (rightly) complains about the high price for drugs we need and then (wrongly) demands price controls. If the government drives down prices, you get shortages. If market competition drives down prices, you get more and better. Everyday examples would be Lasik surgery and mobile phones.

When I started as chief of pediatric cardiology at the University of Chicago in 1990, I decided it would be a good idea for all of our senior team members to have up-to-date technology, that is, mobile phones. Rapid, easy communication can be life-saving when one is dealing with critically ill newborn babies. (Selfishly, I wanted the hospital to be able to get ahold of me when I was out riding long miles, training on my bike.)

Those were the days of the Hewlett Packard "brick" phones. They were the size and weight of a small brick and cost $3,500 each, retail. I gulped at the price and then went outside the University to shop around. I found a private vendor from whom I could get the phones for $1,700 each. While still concerned at the expense of buying six of them, I spoke with the university procurement officer and proudly gave her the good news that, although I was spending $10,200, I was saving the department $10,800.

The officer condescendingly informed me that "the university can't have its faculty going 'rogue' on them." There was a policy and procedure for procurement that had to be followed. "If you want six of those phones, Dr. Waldman, I will get them."

And we did get them, at a cost of $21,000, doing it according to bureaucracy guidelines. Complying with the rules was more important than saving money and avoiding wasteful spending.

The Diagnosis

A part of our healthcare system has gone rogue. It has stopped doing its usual function, which is facilitating the health care of We the Patients. This angel-turned-devil is grabbing all the energy (money) it can find and growing at an alarming rate, apparently without limit.

When that happens inside your body, doctors call it cancer and specify where it started, such as colon cancer or breast cancer. The same is true for a sick system like healthcare.

> # Healthcare diagnosis:
> # Federal Cancer

Antipathy toward Washington has been building over the years. A tongue-in-cheek joke from the internet makes the point.

A University Professor was discussing the Ten Commandments with her students and said they should be applied also to Congress.

For instance, she urged that "honor thy father and thy mother," means we should respect our Representatives and Senators in the Capitol Building. After all, she continued, they are in a sense our mothers and fathers.

One student raised his hand and asked, "Is there a commandment that teaches us what that means, how we should treat politicians in Congress?" Another student immediately shouted out, "Thou shall not kill!"

According to Gallup, the polling service (figure 3-3), Congressional approval ratings in the 1990s were only in the 30–60 percent range, although the nation rallied behind Washington following the 2001 terrorist attacks. Imagine a company whose customers disapproved of how employees treated them most of the time!? That company would quickly be out of business. Not so for Congress, where the re-election rate is consistently greater than 90 percent.

Starting in 2008 and continuing (figure 3-3), Americans have disapproved of our federal Representatives and Senators generally 80 percent, reaching a new record of 91 percent disapproval in 2014.

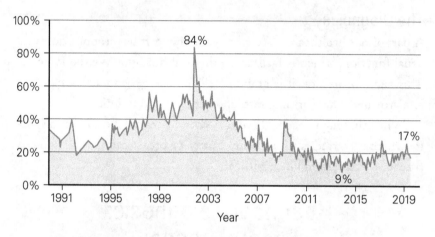

Figure 3-3: Congressional Approval Ratings, 1990 to Present

Washington has become a malignancy in healthcare. Instead of improving our access to care and reducing spending, the federal government and its bureaucracy, using the third-party payment structure, are eating away at the essence of healthcare: patient care.

The cure would seem obvious. Apparently, that is not the case. Some believe the cure for excessive federal control is . . . more government, more control, and more bureaucracy.

Chapter Notes

1. Russell L. Ackoff wrote several books and dozens of helpful articles. However, the best by far is his 1999 *Ackoff's Best: His Classic Writings on Management*. No matter what the reader does personally or professionally, there is much useful wisdom in this book. I urge everyone to read it (and no, I don't get a percentage of the proceeds).

2. A whole chapter is needed to detail bureaucratic diversion in *The Cancer in the American Healthcare System*, another book worth your reading time.

3. John Dunne's phrase came from his Meditation 17, which he wrote in 1624, when he was quite ill with what they called "spotted fever," which could have been any one of a host of viral or even bacterial diseases that cause high fever and skin eruptions. Fortunately, he recovered. While possibly at death's door, he penned these immortal words: "No man is an island, entire of itself; every man is a piece of the continent, a part of the main. If a clod be washed away by the sea, Europe is the less, as well as if a promontory were, as well as if a manor of thy friend's or of thine own were: any man's death diminishes me, because I am involved in mankind, and therefore never send to know for whom the bells tolls; it tolls for thee."

4. Dr. Mary Ruwart's book, *Death by Regulation*, is a chilling tale of the history of the FDA. With solid evidence throughout, the author shows how one federal behemoth costs American lives, suppresses ingenuity and innovation, prevents release of treatments that could save us, and adds trillions (literally) to the price of drugs.

5. Prior to the development of antibiotics, infection was the leading cause of death, accounting for 30 percent of all U.S. deaths in 1900. The creation of ever more powerful, broad-spectrum antibiotics dropped the death rate from infection by 95 percent between 1900 and 1980. That is why they were called "wonder drugs." Sadly, we have become blasé about these potent medicines. While we have been resting on our laurels, bacteria have developed strains resistant to tuberculosis, staphylococcus, and other dangerous germs. With the FDA suppressing new drug development, epidemiologists and clinical physicians have grave concerns.

CHAPTER 4

Single Payer Is Poison, Not Panacea

Some people believe the cure for the sick U.S. healthcare is single payer. They have obviously not read *Single Payer Won't Save Us*.[1] If they had seen that compilation of evidence about single payer systems both in the United States and abroad, they would know it is poison for patients, not a panacea.[2]

Advocates believe the following three claims (falsehoods) regarding single payer healthcare systems. Rather than deciding on faith or being persuaded by others' passion, consider the facts. Let's explode single payer falsehoods.

Single payer has been proven to work.

Have you ever heard of doctors going on strike here in the United States? In 2016, British doctors who work for the vaunted National Health Service (NHS) went out on strike, twice.[3] Further, the British High Court has declared that in life-or-death medical decisions, the hospital can override the family's wishes. That is not what Americans would call an effective, "working," much less compassionate system, and there's worse, much worse, news about single payer.

The single payer NHS, touted by President Obama and ACA architects, is actually medically dangerous. Despite numerous reports of inappropriate care and avoidable deaths, "when the state is a monopoly provider of health care, there is a political interest in suppressing bad news" (such as preventable deaths) regardless of the public's right, indeed, *need* to know.[4]

The single payer system in England tried to use death-by-queueing on my Mum, but we foiled them!

I had two mothers. My natural mother, Mom, was American. My adoptive mother, Mum, was British. She lived just outside Liverpool and worked as a midwife. Of course, she was enrolled in the NHS. When she fell and broke her hip, we assumed the healthcare system would fix it. She was told that she could have hip replacement surgery but had to wait in line until her turn—27 months in the future!

If a 78-year-old, overweight woman were forced to remain immobilized in bed for more than two years, she would likely develop pneumonia, become obese, watch her muscles atrophy, have a blood clot in the lungs (pulmonary embolus), and die long before her surgery. Death-by-queueing.

I discussed this with my British brother, Stewart. I suggested a letter to the NHS requesting prompt surgery on medical grounds for the patient's best interest. Stewart said appealing to altruism wouldn't work, but a financial argument might be heard. Stewart was editor of the *Financial Times*, so he naturally leaned toward the fiscal side.

I composed a letter containing two cost analyses for the NHS: surgery now or surgery in 27 months. (My MBA came in handy.) The former essentially was the expense of the procedure and post-operative rehabilitation. The latter included all the nursing costs, additional medical expenses, and assistive devices for a bed-ridden patient until surgery, plus the operation followed by rehabilitation. Mum had her surgery two months later, went back to work, and lived for another seventeen years.

In Canada's single payer system, patients experience death-by-queueing.[5] A Canadian surgeon, Dr. Ciaran McNamee, sued the Provincial government of Alberta, claiming he had numerous medical records that proved Canadians died waiting in line for care. The fatal delays occurred because their central government restricts allocations for medical equipment and services. There were too few burn units to care for burn victims, and too few surgical suites to operate in time to save patients.

Medicaid, though it functions through middleman insurance companies, also has elements of single payer systems, such as government mandates that determine what care people get and how much providers will be paid. The following describes what Medicaid did to patients.

- **For Want of a Dentist:** In chapter 1, there was the tragic story of Deamonte Driver, who was eligible for government coverage but never got care. While Medicaid is not a typical single payer structure, it is government-controlled healthcare that does not produce adequate access to timely care. As a result, a 12-year-old boy died needlessly and avoidably from complications of an untreated tooth cavity.

- **Death by Waiting:** Illinois expanded its Medicaid program under the ACA. As happened in New Mexico, as noted in chapter 1, expansion increased the number of insured individuals and at the same time increased the wait time for care. Nicholas Horton[6] showed that as a result, 752 Illinoisans died while *in queue*, waiting in line for care.

- **More Medicaid ≠ Better Health:** A study of Medicaid expansion in Oregon[7] showed that Medicaid patients felt less anxious because they had insurance coverage. However, their health outcomes were no better than those who had no insurance at all. Taxpayers paid billions to relieve the worries of Medicaid enrollees but did not improve their physical health.

Studies of healthcare system quality should include individual health outcomes such as cardiac function after heart surgery or mobility after a hip replacement, but most do not. Instead, they use surrogate measures of quality, such as complication rates and communication adequacy. As shown in chapter I, table 1-1, the Commonwealth Fund[8] found that single payer systems were sometimes better than the healthcare system in the United States, and in other respects, they were not.

Single payer systems spend less than the United States

Single payer systems are, in fact, cheaper *for their countries* than is U.S. healthcare, as shown in table 4-1. Whether you consider national spending per capita or as a percentage of GDP, the United States expends much more on healthcare than other nations.

Table 4-1 National Healthcare Spending		
Country	**GDP (%)**	**Per capita**
Canada (SP)	10.9	$4,608
Finland (SP)	9.4	$3,984
Italy (SP)	9.1	$3,272
Japan (SP)	10.3	$4,150
Sweden (SP)	8.8	$5,228
Spain (SP)	8.9	$3,153
UK (SP)	9.1	$4,003
U.S.	17.2	$9,451

SP=Single Payer. GDP=gross domestic product. UK=United Kingdom.

However, when it comes to spending by *individuals or families*, national comparisons become confusing. How people spend money as well as how spending is accounted for vary greatly from country to country. In the United States, payments are made to insurance carriers by individuals or families, or for them by employers or by the government. In 2018, the average American family spent $28,166 on healthcare. That represented 45 percent of their entire income before taxes.

The tax burden in single payer countries is higher than in the United States What is not known is how much of the taxes paid by a Briton, a Swede, or a Canadian is consumed by their single payer healthcare system.

Attempts to study healthcare financing in both single payer nations and the United States discover an opaque—the opposite of transparent—system, where it is virtually impossible to follow the money trail. This is not by accident. Governments do not want people to know precisely where their money is going.

How do single payer systems spend less money than the United States? By rationing, two different ways. Government allocates the amount to be spent on operating rooms or burn units. Such spending is not based on patient needs but on budgetary constraints. Therefore, many burn victims cannot get specialized burn care and some people needing surgery die waiting for an available operating suite.

Single payers also ration care by what they authorize for payment versus what they classify as "not cost effective" and then refuse to authorize. The latter is unavailable even though treatment might save the patient's life.

For example, Great Britain sets age limits on treatments and procedures such as kidney dialysis and heart surgery. If you are too old, the treatment is not authorized. Unless you can pay $125,000 for your coronary bypass or $10,000 per month for dialysis, you die. That is how and why the next belief is not true.

People receive medical care they need with single payer

Supporters of single payer claim that everyone gets the care they need. This is patently false because of strict medical rationing.

In Great Britain, there is an agency that has the most misleading abbreviation I have ever read. NICE, the National Institute for Clinical Excellence, is anything but nice. This agency is tasked with deciding which treatments will be authorized and which will not. Those not authorized for payment effectively become unavailable, because only the very expensive ones are rejected by NICE, and people cannot afford them.

A good example is kidney dialysis, which costs more than $10,000 per month in the United States. In Great Britain's single payer system, kidney dialysis for patients over age 55 years was deemed "not cost effective," and authorization was denied to those over 55. This simple rationing approach did save money at the *cost* of people's lives. Britons died who could have been saved.

You could read the story of Mary Vought's child, who has cystic fibrosis, a genetic disorder that impairs function of the lungs and the intestines. A new drug called Orkambi has been shown to dramatically improve their quality of life, and probably extend lifespan.

While it is still under patent protection, the cost of Orkambi could be as high as $100,000 per year after rebates. Most U.S. commercial insurers cover the bulk of the cost, recognizing that the drug can be life-saving and can save money by avoiding costly hospitalizations.

The British NHS single payer, while admitting Orkambi works, denies patients access to the medication solely on budgetary considerations.[9]

Government control is the reason healthcare is failing patients everywhere. And single payer devotees advocate a system where the government has total control!

The current overregulated structure is wasting our money and denying us the care we need. Yet single payer advocates believe the answer is more regulations.

Government healthcare is poison. Increasing the dose of poison is not good for We the Patients.

Homegrown U.S. single payer

We can observe single payer's bad medical outcomes without ever leaving the United States. Just look at one of our homegrown single payer systems: the Veterans Health Administration system, or VA.

Start with the worst: death-by-queueing. As noted in chapter 1, an internal VA audit of patient outcomes concluded that "47,000 veterans may have died waiting for approval for medical care."

Then there are VA nursing homes. A 2018 expose of VA nursing-home care shows that not only do single payer VA facilities provide substandard care, but the single payer, that is, the federal government, covers it up just like the single payer NHS in Great Britain.

The Centers for Medicare and Medicaid Services (CMS) oversees the care provided to elders in nursing homes, both private and VA. The facilities are required to submit reports with all types of quality measures, such as pain levels, amounts of drugs prescribed, bed sores, hospitalizations and readmissions, infection rates, and deaths. Data from the private facilities is available on a public website. The VA does not share its data with anyone, not even Congress.[10]

In June 2018, reporters from *USA Today* and the *Boston Globe* obtained the embargoed data on quality results in VA nursing homes. Their investigative report showed that, for ten of eleven measures of quality, residents in VA nursing homes throughout the country consistently did worse that residents in private facilities.[11]

The acting secretary of the VA, Peter O'Rourke, released a statement calling the report by *USA Today* and the *Boston Globe* "fake news." Then he refused to release the data that he said would prove his point, that the news was in fact fake.

Single payers fail to provide adequate care and then hide their inadequacies.

A cure that will work

Federal control of healthcare is the root cause of system sickness. The cure for Patient Healthcare is not more federal control, that is, single payer, but the precise opposite: *get Washington out of healthcare.*

What does "get Washington out of healthcare" look like?

Chapter Notes

1.   When released, *Single Payer Won't Save Us* was #4 on the Amazon bestseller list.

2.   Panacea comes from Greek mythology: Panacea was the goddess of universal remedy, a cure-all for everything from a cut finger to cancer. Panacea was the daughter of Epione, the goddess of soothing pain, and Asclepius, son of Apollo and god of healing arts. Another daughter they had was Hygieia. From her name we get the word "hygiene."

3. In April 2016, the Associated Press in London reported, "Thousands of doctors have posted picket lines outside hospitals around England in the first all-out strike in the history of the National Health Service."

4. The following are some of the reports that document scandalous medical outcomes in the NHS: Bristol Royal Infirmary Inquiry, 1994; "Top Doctor's Chilling Claim: The NHS Kills Off 130,000 Elderly Patients Every Year" in *The Daily Mail*, 2012; Morecambe Bay Hospital Report, 2015; "Single-Payer in Crisis: Britain's NHS Cancels 50,000 Surgeries Amid Long Waits For Care, 'Third World' Conditions" in *Townhall*, 2018; Gosport Independent Panel, June 2018; "Great Britain Offers Cautionary Tale on Single Payer" in *Real Clear Health*, 2018; "Reform the NHS Before It Kills Again" in *The Wall Street Journal*, 2018; Edward Baker's 2001 article "Learning from the Bristol Inquiry" in *Cardiology in the Young*; and Ian Kennedy's report "Learning from Bristol: The Report of the Public Inquiry into Children's Heart Surgery at the Bristol Royal Infirmary 1984-1995," presented to Parliament in the United Kingdom by the Secretary of State for Health, July 2001.

5. See chapters 8 and 9 in *The Cancer in the American Healthcare System*, as well as the entire ebook *Single Payer Won't Save Us*.

6. In 2016, Horton published "Hundreds on Medicaid Waiting List in Illinois Die While Waiting for Care."

7. Research on Oregon's "natural social experiment" was published by Baiker et al. in 2013 in the *New England Journal of Medicine*, titled "The Oregon Experiment—Effects of Medicaid on Clinical Outcomes."

8. The Commonwealth Fund report "Mirror, Mirror on the Wall: How the Performance of the U.S. Health Care System Compares Internationally" was published in June 2014.

9. Mary Vought's story about her own child appeared in *USA Today* after President Trump made some unflattering but accurate remarks about the NHS while visiting Great Britain.

10. Following the *USA Today/Boston Globe* exposé, two Senators, Bill Cassidy (R-LA) and Doug Jones (D-AL) had to introduce legislation that would force the VA to release all of the quality data regarding its nursing homes.

11. The report in *USA Today* by Slack and Estes not only summarized the findings but provided the public with the actual VA data, clearly disproving assertions by Acting VA Secretary O'Rourke.

CHAPTER 5
The Cure—StatesCare

With the root cause of healthcare failure clearly in mind—*cancer*—the fix or cure is straightforward: remove the cancer.[1] Since the cancer is an overgrown, overbearing, massively overspending federal bureaucracy, the cure is to cut down the bureaucracy to a manageable size.

But how can this be done? Some say it is impossible. If you agree that healthcare cannot be fixed, you guarantee that it never will be fixed. You have created a self- fulfilling prophecy.

If we wait for Washington to fix healthcare, we will wait forever. It was Washington that created and continuously expanded its healthcare bureaucracy. Federal politicians are either unwilling or unable to accept the truth. They, their rules, regulations, and mandates are the problem. Therefore, they, their rules, regulations, and mandates can never be the solution.

Chief Justice Roberts of the Supreme Court wrote that federal Medicaid mandates "undermine the status of the States as independent sovereigns in our federal system." And in the landmark NFIB (National Federation of Independent Business) case that upheld Obamacare, Justice Roberts noted, "...we look to the States to defend their prerogatives by adopting 'the simple expedient of not yielding' to federal blandishments (money) when they do not want to embrace the federal policies as their own."[2] If a state doesn't like federal Medicaid mandates, that state shouldn't take federal Medicaid money.

Washington politicians are likely to resist giving up control of one sixth of our economy. Their expansion of federal bureaucracy has created loyal federal bureaucrats who support Washington, will vote for the people who gave them jobs, and don't want to lose their high-paying positions.[3]

The desire to control healthcare is bipartisan. Both parties are guilty of power hunger. While Republicans claim they want to reduce the size of government, President Ronald Reagan, a paragon of conservatism, expanded the federal bureaucracy.[4] The Democrats have repeatedly demonstrated their intent to federalize healthcare, from President Johnson's Great Society to the ACA and now, the dishonestly named Medicare-for-All (which abolishes Medicare)!

Strategic plan

Most people believe that strategic planning is only for military operations. In fact, every time you want to accomplish anything, from manufacturing a car to hiring a new employee to buying a candy bar, you need a strategic plan to reach your goal.

Curing healthcare is our goal. We need a strategic plan to achieve it. The first step is to identify the result we want. As Stephen Covey advised everyone, "Start with the end in mind." The end—the desired outcome—should be what you truly want, not what you think is practicable or politically possible.

America was built on the idea that *free Americans can do anything*. Freedom combined with capitalism releases our potential. Anything is possible, including a healthcare system that works for We the Patients.

The end we seek is *timely, quality health care chosen by the patient at a cost that both individuals and the nation can afford*. THAT is the goal of our strategic plan.

Both managers and doctors have a similar piece of wisdom on the timing of a strategic plan. Physicians know the sicker a patient is, the faster you must heal him. Managers know that the more radical the change needed, the faster you should make it happen. If you do things slowly, incrementally, while avoiding shocks to the system, the forces of status quo will get organized and stop the change. In the ER, if you do things very slowly, incrementally, while avoiding any shocks, the auto accident victim will bleed to death.

In other words, a massive change like getting the federal government out of healthcare should be accomplished over years, not generations.

An effective strategy enlists the people involved rather than being imposed on them from above. That is particularly true of Americans. We prize our freedom over goodies the government promises to deliver but never does. "A government big enough to give you everything you want, is a government big enough to take away everything that you have."[5]

One reason people resist Obamacare is the fact that President Obama imposed his namesake law on citizens against our will. Even if it were "for our own good" (it isn't), we still would resist because it denies us the freedom to choose for ourselves.

While a strategy for radical change must move quickly, Americans must be deeply involved in the design and development, engaged in the process, educated about what it means to them personally, and enthusiastic for what is going to happen.

A problem is only permanently fixed when the root cause is gone. For healthcare, curing the cancer means getting Washington out of healthcare. Healthcare decisions should be made by the people, We the Patients, not by Washington politicos and their henchman (and -woman) bureaucrats. That is what we call StatesCare.[6]

StatesCare transfers the organization, financing, administration, and regulation (what little is necessary) of healthcare to the people in their states. Representing their people, state legislators decide the healthcare structure best suited to their people's needs and state resources.

Don't get sucked in to the false narrative that the states are dependent on federal dollars. The only money Washington has is the money We the People give it. The states would rather spend their tax dollars on healthcare as they see fit, than as some federal bureaucrat tells them they must.

There may be incremental, intermediate steps along the way to getting Washington totally out of healthcare, but the end goal should always be kept clearly in mind and out in the open.

It is unlikely that Washington will easily relinquish authority over healthcare to the states until there is a massive groundswell felt at the ballot box and/or from a convention of states.[7]

Waivers

Recently, there has developed enthusiasm for waivers of federal mandates, particularly for Medicaid, as a way of getting around the administrative and regulatory burdens imposed by Washington.

Essentially every federal act contains a process by which a state can request a variance from what the law says. This process, called a waiver, is intended to allow the state to demonstrate that there is an alternative approach, different from what the law mandates, that can achieve better results.[8] Waivers are generally named for their section numbers within the law.

For example, the original Medicaid law of 1965 contains Section 1115 that allows a state to waive federal Medicaid regulations specified in the waiver request. State waivers must be approved by the relevant federal agency. For healthcare, that is the Centers for Medicare & Medicaid Services (CMS).

Medicaid programs are failing throughout the nation. They are devouring state resources,[9] providing inadequate access to care,[10] and producing *worse* medical outcomes than no insurance at all![11]

Medicaid programs are failing in part because of "mission creep": the original goals have been distorted or lost. Medicaid was conceived as a program for those who are "unable," that is, aged, blind, or disabled. It was initially focused on those who would literally *die* without government support for their medical care. Medicaid now covers perfectly healthy, able-bodied persons up through 25 years of age as well as senior citizen services that Medicare does not cover.

According to the 1965 Medicaid law, state programs were supposed to be state-administered, not run by Washington. Piece by piece, adding new rules to old ones and expanding program parameters, Washington has taken over administration of all state programs. From eligibility standards and verification processes to benefit packages and even pricing, Washington dictates (mandates) and states must obey.

Following is a partial list of the federal legislation that expanded state Medicaid programs:[12]

- Social Security Amendments of 1967
- Employee Retirement Income Security Act of 1974
- Tax Equity and Fiscal Responsibility Act of 1982
- Omnibus Budget Reconciliation Act of 1985
- Omnibus Budget Reconciliation Act of 1987
- Medicare Catastrophic Coverage Act of 1988
- Omnibus Budget Reconciliation Act of 1990
- National Breast and Cervical Cancer Early Detection Program of 1991
- Omnibus Budget Reconciliation Act of 1992
- Omnibus Budget Reconciliation Act of 1993
- Omnibus Budget Reconciliation Act of 2003.

Washington uses a command-and-control, one-size-fits-all approach that is applied equally across a continent more than 3000 miles wide containing 327 million people.

Rhode Island and Montana have identical numbers of residents, 1.06 million. Rhode Island has 5146 physicians within 1212 square miles. Montana has 1100 physicians scattered over 145,000 square miles. There are three world-famous university hospitals less than one hour's drive from Providence, Rhode Island. The nearest major medical facility/trauma center to Helena, Montana, is in Salt Lake City, Utah, more than 8 hours' drive away, assuming the roads are passable.

It is both illogical and unrealistic to think that the same set of insurance rules and healthcare mandates will work in Rhode Island as in Montana, yet that is how Washington operates.

More than fifteen states have asked for waivers in Medicaid or the ACA so they can circumvent restrictive federal mandates and tailor their programs to the specific needs of their consumers and the limitations on their resources.

Waivers are a trap. They continue to recognize federal authority where it should not exist. Americans should not have to ask for federal approval to decide their healthcare. We the Patients should be free to do so without a permission slip from the feds.

Beware! Caution! Warning!

When politicians shout, "Trust us!"; when media talking heads solemnly intone, "Better the devil we know than the one we don't"; and when fear of change threatens your resolve to do what you know is right, keep this in mind. With StatesCare, we won't be giving $1.4 trillion "healthcare" dollars to Washington. Those 1,400,000,000,000 dollars can be used to pay for patient care without costing you an extra penny.

Legal basis for StatesCare

The Tenth Amendment to the U.S. Constitution reads, "The powers not delegated to the United States by the Constitution, nor prohibited by it to the States, are reserved to the States respectively, or to the people." Healthcare was not a power delegated to the federal government, and thus healthcare was reserved to the states and to the people.

The Founding Fathers of our country did not simply "forget" about healthcare. Five signatories on the Declaration of Independence as well as numerous delegates to the Constitutional Convention were physicians.

State or popular control of healthcare was reaffirmed by the great jurist Chief Justice John Marshall in 1824 (*Gibbon v. Ogden*): "health laws of every description" are reserved to the states.

Section 1801 of the 1965 Medicaid law is titled "Prohibition against any federal interference." The authors clearly intended for all Medicaid programs to be administered locally, that is, by the states. However, over five decades, the federal government has taken over every aspect of 51 Medicaid programs that were supposed to be run locally rather than centrally.

In 2012, even as he protected the Obamacare law from legal challenge, Chief Justice Roberts reminded us that states are "sovereign entities" that can choose to ignore federal healthcare mandates by simply saying no to federal bribery.

Even though the waiver process may seem the most politically viable option, many Americans recoil from the necessity. They believe the individual, not the government, should be free to decide his or her own health care. One should not have to ask permission from Washington to exercise a freedom that should be theirs in the first place.

What if?

If StatesCare were available, what might We the People do with our new-found freedom? Is a market-based approach possible? What might it look like? Read on.

Chapter Notes

1. For the complete explanation from symptoms to diagnosis of root cause, read *The Cancer in the American Healthcare System.*

2. The quote can be found on page 49 of Supreme Court case *National Federation of Independent Business v. Sebelius, Secretary of Health and Human Services*, No. 11–393, June 28, 2012.

3. Federal bureaucrats are paid 78 percent more than private-sector workers doing the same jobs. In 2014, federal compensation averaged $119,934, while average income in the private sector was $67,246.

4. There is debate on this issue, depending on a person's political leaning. Reagan's detractors say that spending increased, while his supporters point to his taking authority from the bureaucratic "state" and returning it to the legislative branch.

5. Like many individuals, I thought Thomas Jefferson said this. Apparently, I was wrong. The first appearance of this quote was found in Paul Harvey's 1952 book *Remember These Things*, 126 years after the death of Jefferson.

6. I have been suggesting the idea of StatesCare in different ways for years in various publications, such as

    -   *The Hill*, Nov. 12, 2016. "The Great Disruptor Can Fix Healthcare."

    -   *FoxNews.com*, Jan. 4, 2017. "A Doctor's Straight Talk: America, Your Health Care Is Not a Federal Responsibility."

- *Washington Examiner*, March 23, 2017. "Instead of the House Healthcare Bill, Replace Federal Healthcare Laws by Letting the States Decide What to Do."

- The *Daily Caller*, May 4, 2017. "Let States Have Their Own Healthcare Systems."

- *The Hill*, Nov. 30, 2017. "ObamaCare Contributed to the Murder of Health Care, But It's —Not the Only Culprit."

- *Op-Ed News*, June 16, 2019. "Washington Should Leave Healthcare to States."

7. Article 5 of the U.S. Constitution shows how the people can force a recalcitrant Congress to do what the people want. It reads as follows. "The Congress . . . shall propose Amendments to this Constitution, or, on the *Application of the Legislatures of two thirds of the several States* [italics added for emphasis], shall call a Convention for proposing Amendments, which . . . shall be valid to all Intents and Purpose." With current Congressional approval ratings hovering in the teens, enthusiasm for a convention of states is increasing. In fact, as of January 2018, 27 states have passed resolutions calling for redress of government overreach using Article 5. When the number of states reaches 34, a convention will be called, according to our Constitution.

8. My 2019 article with Jennifer Minjarez, "Extend Gains from Welfare Reform to Texas Medicaid," shows how the waiver process can be used to improve the Medicaid program in the Lone Star State.

9. Read how Medicaid spending is consuming state resources that are needed for education, infrastructure, or border security, in "The Saga of 1115—A Waiver Can Fix Texas Medicaid, But Only Temporarily," published through Texas Public Policy Foundation, March 2017.

10. A 2017 survey by Merritt Hawkins showed that expanded Medicaid enrollment due to the ACA increased the wait time for a patient to see a family physician by more than four months!

11. Reports by LaPar (2010), Ellis (2017), and Younossi (2018) demonstrate substandard outcomes in Medicaid patients after surgery, with cancer, and infected with Hepatitis C respectively.

12. See my article "ObamaCare Contributed to the Murder of Health Care, but It's Not the Only Culprit," in *The Hill*, November 2017.

CHAPTER 6
Market-Based Medicine

States free to fix healthcare should *not* begin by asking what is practical or likely to get Congressional approval. Political expedience is *not* a proper starting point. You start by saying what you want.

What Americans want is a healthcare system where people are free to choose their caregivers as well as their care; free to decide how to spend their money; and free from some third party—government or insurance carrier—making medical as well as financial decisions for them.

Federal control of healthcare and third-party payment is inconsistent with three founding principles of the United States: (1) It stifles freedom. In fact, it returns us to a tyranny we rejected nearly 250 years ago; (2) The deadly duo of federal control and third-party decision-making rejects personal responsibility. Others are in charge. Others are responsible; and (3) According to the Tenth Amendment to the Constitution, healthcare is clearly "reserved to the states respectively, or to the people."[1]

Healthcare never was and is not now a federal responsibility.[2]

Washington has been likened to a swamp, one that controls us by taking charge of our money. To fix healthcare, we need to drain the swamp. We need to get Washington OUT of healthcare and return authority to We the Patients in our states.

In 2017, the CEO of a medium-sized Texas company called the main desk at the Texas Public Policy Foundation in Austin demanding "to speak with someone who knew what in blazes is going on with healthcare and who could do something about it!" At that time, I was working at the Foundation. The intern called my office and hesitantly asked if I would speak with the irate caller. Of course, I said yes.

When we were connected, he asked who I was, and then without waiting for my answer, he began regaling me with complaints he had heard from several of his employees. One man received a surprise bill after an ER visit at a facility where his care was supposedly covered by his health plan. Another employee had a child whose doctor wanted a second opinion, but the insurance agents kept giving excuses why this could not be done. A third employee needed a medication prescribed by her doctor, but the insurance company's pharmacy benefits manager repeatedly denied prescriptions the doctor wrote.

The CEO continued, "Why am I paying all this money to insurance companies if my people can't get the care they need? Am I just throwing hundreds of thousands of dollars in the toilet?!"

After taking two deep, cleansing breaths (I shared his outrage but had to sound calm), I began to explain. "Healthcare has a third-party payment system, not the free market you are used to. The third-party insurance company that pays for goods and services has a strong incentive *not* to provide service. That is why they delay, defer, or deny care," I continued.

When I tried to show him how this hurt his employees, he again interrupted me, exclaiming, "That's the dumbest thing I ever heard! Who invented such a stupid system?" he asked. "Congress," I replied. Then, without knowing anything about systems theory or good medical practice, and lacking my years of studying and analyzing our healthcare system, the CEO came up with the correct answer.

"Hell, son, that's easy. We should just tell Washington and them third parties to go [***crude expletives and anatomically impossible commands deleted***]. Kick them out of the way and create our own system. We damned sure could do a better job than those idiots in D.C.!!"

Without knowing the term for it, the CEO was colorfully advocating what I call market-based medicine.[3]

StatesCare

StatesCare has one huge financial advantage that is so obvious, it might be missed. With StatesCare, the states will be fiscally responsible. They will stay within budget and not spend more than they can afford.

With Washington in charge of healthcare, federal politicians invariable expand the bureaucracy with its huge additional costs and divert more money away from patient care. The states won't do this. Washington can spend more money than we pay in taxes for one reason—the treasury can print new dollars. The states can't. They will stay within their budgets because they have to!

What should states do with their newfound, or more accurately, their restored Tenth Amendment independence from Washington? They should do whatever they think best for their people. States are more familiar with the local needs and more responsive to their constituents than are federal legislators.

Media reports have suggested what some states might choose for healthcare.

Californians appear to favor a single payer structure similar to Great Britain's National Health Service.[4] The Golden State has 2 million more people than the whole country of Canada, where there is a single payer structure. Shouldn't California be entitled to have its own system? Should the District of Columbia tell 39 million Californians they must do what Washington mandates?

A compilation of facts about single payer systems is available in the e-book *Single Payer Won't Save Us*. Based on the evidence, I have concluded that single payer is a bad choice. However, I do not live in California. Neither I nor federal politicians should tell Californians what they should do.

Vermont hired Jonathan Gruber, one of the architects of the ACA, as a consultant. He assured them they could have a single payer healthcare system all by themselves. When the cost became known, the Vermont legislature dropped the idea and demanded their $400,000 consulting fee back from Gruber.[5]

Washington state seems to want their own form of universal health care.[6] This would be taxpayer-funded, free-at-point-of-service health care where there is a government approved list of available treatments from which providers can choose.

Another state option might be to emulate the German system of regionalized care for every citizen.[7] The availability of care for noncitizens would be decided by that state.

Is there a healthcare model controlled by free-market forces, a market-based system? Does any country have such a system? Healthcare in Switzerland and Singapore does include some market forces. However, these systems are still controlled by a central authority rather than the decentralized decision making process inherent in a free market.

So, is market-based healthcare truly impossible, or is it a dream that American ingenuity has not yet made real?

Market-based medicine

There are two ways to structure a market: central control or decentralized.

In a centralized system, decisions about supply, demand, and prices are made by the government, federal or state. Single payer, universal health care, socialized medicine, and Obamacare are forms of a centrally controlled healthcare. There are reams of data about the results with these forms of a centralized market.

In a decentralized market, decisions about supply and demand are made by millions of consumers and sellers, one by one. Price is a signaling mechanism between buyer and seller. There is no data about decentralizing the market in healthcare.

Two widespread misconceptions have prevented the idea of market-based healthcare from gaining traction: (1) health care is a right; and (2) market failure is the reason that the U.S. healthcare system doesn't work. Health care as a *right* was debunked in chapter 2. What about so-called market failure?

The United States has not had a free market in healthcare since the advent of third-party payment in the 1930s. A free market has only two parties, buyer and seller, who are directly connected by a commercial exchange. The seller provides services and goods in exchange for the buyer's money. The buyer has a strong incentive to economize and sellers must compete for buyers' dollars.

For almost everything in day-to-day life, Americans live in a free-market economy. Whether one is buying food or a house or purchasing legal services or dry cleaning, there is one buyer and one seller, with no third party in between. Buyers decide the best value (price and quality) for them and pay the seller for the product or service chosen. The seller decides what combination of price and quality will attract buyers' dollars.

It may seem perfunctory to write the above, but it is so much a part of our lives that we do not even think about this process. Introducing a third-party as the decision maker changes everything. By disconnecting buyer from seller, third party payment turns a free market into a controlled market.

Some people believe the rise of third-party payment systems occurred *in response* to the high cost of care. In fact, it was the other way around! Escalation in the cost of care was caused by the disconnection of patient/buyer from provider/seller by the third party: insurance companies and federal government.

Third-party payment is not sustainable without strict medical rationing. Those who consume services and goods don't pay the bill. Those who provide care don't determine the price. A financing structure devoid of buyers' incentive to economize and sellers' need to compete for buyers' dollars is inherently unstable. Predictably, prices go up with no end in sight, and shortages get worse. That is exactly what Americans have experienced. Supply and demand can be balanced only by the government, using price and wage controls and medical rationing.

Two causes of healthcare system failure are thus inextricably interwoven. Federal bureaucracy and its inefficiency sap the lifeblood of healthcare: money. Federal rules and regulations suppress free-market forces and protect the third-party payment structure.

Principles

In 1776, the United States of America replaced a failing, centrally controlled *political system* with one based on individual freedom. Today, we need to replace a failing, centrally controlled *healthcare system*, but with what? We would do well to follow our Founding Fathers. Let's start by enunciating foundational principles.

The following are my recommended primary tenets for an effective and efficient, uniquely American market-based healthcare system. They are listed in order of importance.

1. Freedom: Healthcare must not impinge on Americans' liberty, their right to choose.

2. Personal Responsibility: With freedom comes personal responsibility, including responsibility for our health.

3. Dollar Efficiency: Most healthcare dollars should pay for care and the least should go to noncare activities such as administration, bureaucracy, regulation, and compliance.

4. Safety Net: The system should be designed for the majority of Americans. A safety net should be included for those unable to provide for their own medical needs.

5. Prioritization: Support for the healthcare system must fit within all public priorities.

Patient and doctor are directly connected

Several years ago, I had just finished a cardiac procedure on a baby at the Children's Hospital and was walking back to my office to change out of my green scrubs. The corridor was very long, very quiet, and empty of people.

Well, not quite. There was a small child, probably 18 months old, in sandals, walking—or more accurately, strolling—down the corridor by himself. He was intently inspecting the doors and equipment. No parents. No doctors, nurses, or patients—just this little boy and me.

I walked up to him and softly asked if I might walk with him. He considered my offer, then raised his hand and took my fingers. No fear, no stranger-danger. Just him and me.

We slowly walked together until reaching my office. In there, the brightly colored objects and toys immediately grabbed his attention. He released me and began to explore. I sat down and called Security. The parents were there, frantic, but relieved when I said Alex (I learned his name) was fine. I said they could come to my office to collect their intrepid explorer child.

After they arrived, and following a group hug, all three went on their way.

When I said there was no one with Alex and me in the corridor, I forgot to mention the photographer. As Alex and I were walking together, a man with a camera came from the opposite direction and stopped us. He explained that he was taking promotional pictures for the hospital and asked, "Could I take your picture?" I turned to ask Alex and he nodded. I then reminded the photographer that he would need a signed release from the parents. He agreed and took our picture.

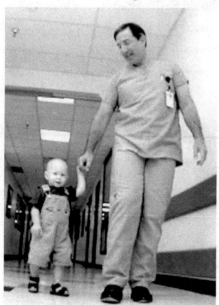

Figure 6-1: Connect Directly with the Patient

Figure 6-1 shows the two of us. This picture became the front cover of the Children's Hospital annual report. It is the epitome of the patient-doctor relationship with no one, nothing, no third payer, no government bureaucrat in between.

Our current healthcare system is designed to *disconnect* the patient from the doctor. Federal mandates and insurance rules build administrative, regulatory, and compliance "walls" that separate Alex, the patient, from me, the doctor (figure 6-2).

Figure 6-2: Disconnection of Patient from Doctor

Such disconnection of buyer from seller, patient from personal physician, turns the government bureaucrat and the insurance agent into the medical and financial decision maker for you, me, and every American. The healthcare system fails to provide timely, affordable care. We are not in control of our lives or our money. Claiming to know what is best for us, others are in charge of us. There is no free market, or freedom for that matter.

To create a functioning marketplace for health care, reestablish the fiduciary service relationship, *reconnect buyer with seller*, patient directly with doctor, with no third party in between.

Patient is buyer, consumer, and payer

Suppose you are thinking about buying a car. After looking at your bank account, you decide how much you can afford to spend. The federal government can print money to spend, but you can't.

Your car choices are Ford, Honda, and Mercedes. You activate a car-buying program on the internet and look up various models. You place them side by side on the screen. You compare price, maintenance costs, resale value, miles per gallon, and other features. You test drive the vehicles, decide which is the best value, and buy the car. You know you can afford the monthly payments because you first checked the cost compared to your monthly income and other obligations.

Switch focus to buying health care within a market-based system. You want a doctor for yourself or a pediatrician for your child, which means you want to purchase the care provider's services. You activate a medical shopping internet program and search for doctors within easy access. You refine your search based on price, wait times, years of experience, type of practice, satisfaction surveys, and even gender of the provider. You narrow the list to three individuals and go visit them. (You are taking them for a test drive.) You get a price list from the doctor for services you want or might need in the future. You check the funds in your health savings account (HSA). You decide which doctor provides the best value and contract with that physician.

The federal government plays no role (figure 6-3). Washington doesn't tell you what car to buy or which doctor to choose. A federal bureaucrat doesn't say which automobile features or what insurance you must purchase. An insurance agent does not tell you how long you will wait to get your car or your medical care. Even validation of miles per gallon and customer satisfaction surveys is done by independent, private companies.

Figure 6-3: Market-Based Medicine Is Simple

There is an important distinction between buying an automobile and purchasing health care. You don't *need* a high-priced Mercedes car. If you can't afford it, the lower-priced Honda or Ford will provide dependable, affordable transportation.

But when you have a heart attack, you really *do* need that very expensive operation and ICU stay. Nothing less will do. Without them, you die. That is why you buy high-deductible insurance: to protect against the financial catastrophe of an unexpected large medical bill—an auto accident or a surprise heart attack.

Many of the expensive and so-called unexpected medical events can and should be *anticipated*. A patient who is a diabetic could shop in advance for a hospital, which may be needed in the event of a collapse from too much or too little sugar in the blood. A 350-pound patient with a family history of heart disease, a high-stress job, and a cholesterol level of 400 could and should discuss with his or her doctor where to go when the inevitable occurs. Plan in advance for the doctor and hospital you want!

Figure 6-4: HSA Replaces All of Healthcare

High-priced, dramatic medical events like an auto crash or cancer make eye-catching headlines and even book titles, but a healthcare system should not be constructed primarily for the uncommon events.

A sustainable, effective healthcare system should be designed first to handle common medical problems such as infections, rashes, diarrhea, sugar control in diabetics, asthma, blood pressure maintenance, delivering babies, arthritis, and minor trauma. The cash in HSAs would easily cover these expenses without any insurance involvement, especially with the lower prices produced by market forces. Big-ticket items like brain or heart surgery are what high-deductible insurance is for.

Sellers determine price

In any decentralized or "free" market, consumers determine demand. (In today's centrally controlled healthcare system, Washington and insurance companies do that.) In an unrestricted market, sellers decide prices and consumers are free to pay one seller's price, find a lower-priced seller, or just say no.

In market-based healthcare, the lower-priced hospital or physician will get more of consumers' business as long as consumers believe there is requisite value.

If you need a hernia repair in a market-based system, you compare prices and outcomes before you buy. For instance, a university hospital has done 1000 such procedures with a 95 percent success rate at a cost of $12,043. The Surgical Center of Oklahoma (SCO, Table 6-2), a cash-only, no-insurance facility, has done 450 such repairs with a 92 percent success rate at a cost of $5750. You, the consumer, decide whether the 3 percent difference is worth $6293.

Note that both price (consumer's cost) and results are automatically transparent in a market-based system.

Incentives: perverse and aligned

Incentives, positive or negative, affect behavior. If you reward A more than B, you will get more of A and less of B.[8] If you punish C and do not punish D, you know what will happen.

A *perverse* incentive rewards the outcome you *don't want*, and so, you get more of what you don't want. If you reward your child for every "F" he or she gets in school, soon the student will flunk out. This is what healthcare has—perverse incentives. Hospital executives get big bonuses when they balance their budgets by cutting services. We reward politicians' promises by re-electing them, even when they fail to make good on those promises. So, next election, they make more false promises, don't deliver, and return to Washington.

An *aligned* incentive rewards the outcome you *do want*. What consumers want from the healthcare system is *care*. Yet insurance companies make more money when they delay, defer, or deny the care we need now. The federal government expands its bureaucracy, which increases inefficient healthcare spending and leaves less money for patient care.

By removing the third party, insurance or government, we reconnect patients with doctors *directly*. Incentives are automatically aligned. Consumers pay for what they want—care—and therefore get what they want. Sellers who offer better value will be rewarded with what they want: profit.

DISCLAIMER

Calculations that follow are for demonstartion purposes only. They offer proof of concept. They are AN answer but not necessarily THE answer for you and your state.

One size truly does *not* fit all.

We the People know best— We the People should decide.

How much will it cost me?!

In 2018, the average American family of four spent $28,166 on healthcare expenses, mostly for insurance premiums, plus deductibles and co-pays.[9]

Most people see this as a sign of failure of the U.S. healthcare system, and it certainly is! However, I also see it as a great opportunity.

I think to myself, "Suppose individual Americans, instead of Washington politicians, controlled their own money. What would they do (figure 6-5)?!"

The typical family is healthy and would need to expend only a small amount annually out of their HSA for medical care. If contributions to the HSA were unlimited and the account were allowed to accrue, a typical family would soon have a very large sum in their HSA. There would be enough money to pay for almost any form of care short of open-heart surgery, especially with lower prices for care in a free-market environment (Table 6-2).

Figure 6-5: What Should We Do with Half Our Income?!

Obtaining health care would be just like shopping for any product or service. The consumer (patient or buyer) chooses among sellers (doctors or therapists) and pays for care from an HSA. Consumers know in advance the exact price they will pay and what services they will get. Doctors know what they will be paid, when, and what the patient expects. Doctors who overcharge or do not deliver prompt service will find their waiting rooms and bank accounts empty.

Individuals spend their own money rather than other people's money and have "skin in the game." However, some modern, high-tech health care can be very expensive and beyond most people's pocketbooks. That is why people would purchase high-deductible insurance.

The answer to "How much will it cost me?" is an affordable price, a small fraction of what you are mandated to pay now.

Rules

Market-based healthcare was designed to be true to its founding principles. It is applicable to the general population, with a safety net added as described following. The system has four simple rules:

1. Money in an HSA can be used only for medical* expenses.
2. The HSA holder can expend HSA funds for anyone's medical care, including nonfamily members.
3. Unused HSA funds can accumulate indefinitely.
4. While purchasing high-deductible insurance is strongly encouraged, it is not mandatory in a market-based system.

---

* Medical expenses are determined by patients, not by the government. Cost effectiveness is decided by the consumer, not an ACA panel.[10] If a patient wants nontraditional medical care, such as acupuncture, crystal treatments, or aromatherapy, that is the patient's decision. As long as HSA funds are not used to buy cigarettes, alcohol, or a big-screen TV—in other words, as long as spending is medical as the patient defines "medical,"—there are no government-mandated restrictions on HSA use.

Insurance

Years ago, in New Mexico, I had a one-month-old patient with a rare and complex heart problem. There were very few doctors who could operate on babies like her. One surgeon in California had much higher survival rates than anyone else in the country. I wanted to send my patient there. The baby was covered by a Medicaid insurance contract with a different hospital, where the results in patients like mine were not as good. The medical director of the insurance company refused to let me send the baby where she had the best chance to survive. He wouldn't budge.

The baby's father found a solution. He would simply transfer her insurance to one that would send her to California. However, there was a big problem. Insurance rules allowed him to transfer insurance only when the baby was an out-patient, meaning not in the hospital. The baby needed a medication that could be given only inside the hospital. If I let her go home, I had to stop the IV drug and she might die.

I discharged the baby at about 6 o'clock at night on a Tuesday and brought her back into the hospital around 6 o'clock the next morning. Fortunately, she was still okay without the IV medicine. During that time, the father had transferred the child's insurance. A week later, she had her surgery in California and did well.

While the transfer team was getting her ready to fly to California, the neonatologist and I were on the other side of a curtain divider. She asked me if I knew how much trouble I was in for discharging the baby. I said, "Yes, but I *had* to do it!" As the transfer team was leaving with baby and parents, the mother stopped me. She obviously had heard what the neonatologist said. With tears in her eyes and giving me a hug, she whispered, "Thank you for my baby."

In market-based healthcare, insurance returns to its original function: protection against financial catastrophe. Insurance carriers no longer make medical decisions.

In a free-market environment, sellers of insurance compete for consumers' dollars. Since they pay out of pocket for their own care, consumers can decide their care. In a centrally controlled "market" such as we have now, the "customers" of insurance sellers are really the health plans or the government, not the consumers. Since the third parties are the payers, they decide the care.

In the proposed market-based system, insurance carriers can offer for sale whatever policies they think consumers want. Policies might include contracts with medical facilities for fixed prices, as they do now. Carriers might also choose to sell policies that pay whatever price the patient has accepted, after the patient pays the high deductible. This means the majority of care would be paid for from patients' HSAs and not insurance carriers.

In market-based healthcare, those with pre-existing conditions will, like everyone else, be paying for care first out of their HSAs. They too will have reason to economize and seek the best prices. This works to their advantage (obviously) but also works to the advantage of the insurance company. The money paid out by the chronically ill from their HSAs is money the insurance company does not have to pay. The actuarial cost to the insurance carrier of those with pre-existing conditions will be reduced, and therefore, insurance sellers can sell their policies at much lower prices that in the present system. The big-ticket, super-expensive heart surgeries and auto crash victims make great headlines and sell books, but they are uncommon and comprise only a small fraction of healthcare spending. For every open-heart operation, there are tens of thousands of cases of diarrhea, pneumonia, arthritis, urinary tract infections, minor trauma, out-patient surgery, and routine check-ups. Insurance carriers pay for none of these in a market-based system.

In summary, consumers pay for care up to their deductible limit, which should be very high, say $5,000 or preferably $10,000. The cost of such catastrophic, high-deductible insurance would be a fraction of current prices. We estimate $5,000 a year or less for a family of four rather than the more than $18,000 the family paid in premiums in 2018.[11]

When healthcare is market based, consumers dictate price and quality. Most important, patients, not the federal government, determine their medical care.

Consumers Know Best; Father (Washington) does not.

Effects

Market-based healthcare will have positive effects on both We the Patients and Americans' dollars. Sellers of goods and services will be forced to compete. Prices will plummet when market forces are allowed to function.

Lasik (laser) surgery for cataracts was approved in the United States in 1999. At that time, the cost was $4500 per eye. By 2019, free-market forces drove down the cost to consumers to $220 per eye, a decrease of more than 95 percent within twenty years.

Contrast third-party insurance or government payer with cash-only, no-third-party, direct-pay medicine in the United States, also called market-based medicine. When healthcare is market-based, the hassle and cost of insurance administration as well as federal compliance simply . . . vanishes.

Data from direct-pay practices shows that costs to consumers go down while payments to providers go up. In Table 6-1, note that Medicaid pays from 22 to 54 percent of the doctor's charges. The billed charges of the direct-pay practice are consistently *lower* than insurance. Yet the doctor gets paid more in every instance. Elimination of third-party insurance or government involvement produces better and cheaper care at the same time.

In a market where sellers compete for consumers' dollars, sellers will have to display their prices openly. Those who do not will quickly be out of business. With market-based healthcare, transparency will replace the hidden (opaque) price structure of the current third-party payment system.

With market-based healthcare, spending will go down, both for individuals and for the nation. When people spend their own money, they have "skin in the game." With a powerful incentive to economize, personal spending declines. StatesCare eliminates the huge cost of federal BARRCO: bureaucracy, administration, rules, regulations, compliance, and oversight.[12] More than one trillion dollars of federal "healthcare" spending either disappears or is converted to payments for patient care.[13] Either way, We the Patients win.

Table 6-1: Market-based Prices* versus Third-Party Charges and Medicaid Payments (2018)

Procedure	Average Total Charges		Average Total Payment	
	Univ. Hosp.	SCO	SCO	Medicaid
Childbirth, vaginal	$4,719	$3,111	$3,111	$2,557
Cataract surgery, one eye	$7,390	$4,000	$4,000	$1,637
Laparoscopic repair, inguinal hernia, one side	$12,043	$5,750	$5,750	$3,157
Hip replacement, one side	$35,114	$15,499	$15,499	$12,922

(*) In market-based medicine, price and payment are the same; in third-party payment, they are usually different. Univ. Hosp.=University of New Mexico Health Sciences Center; payments vary according to contract with specific insurance carrier. SCO=Surgery Center of Oklahoma, Oklahoma City, OK, a no-insurance, cash-only surgical facility. Medicaid is used as a typical example of federally determined payment schedules.

As written repeatedly, a healthcare system should be focused first on *care*, and on money only after patients get the care they need. A free market in healthcare will increase patients' access to care. The market, not the federal government, will decide how much providers are paid, which will be much more than government reimbursement schedules. They receive payment at time of service, without the hassle, expense, and delay associated with the complex federal billing, coding, review, and payment process.

The net effects of changing from third-party-payment to market-based medicine will be uniformly salutary (figure 6-6). Prices and spending will decline. Payments to providers will increase. When providers are paid more, when they compete for consumers' *business* and are released from administrative and regulatory burdens, patients' access to care and time with the doctor will increase greatly.

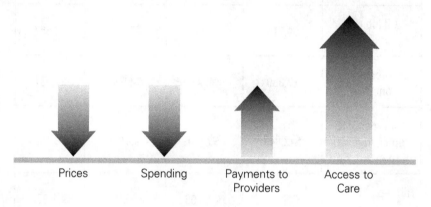

Prices   Spending   Payments to   Access to
                                    Providers   Care

Figure 6-6: Effects of Market-Based Medicine

Medicare-for-All, H.R. 1384, is being proposed as a solution for our healthcare dilemma. This act will eliminate all market forces, supposedly remove profit motive, and prevent private insurance and even the private practice of medicine. Medicare-for-All and its follow-on bill, Medicare for America, achieve total central control of healthcare by the federal government.

The now-defunct Union of Soviet Socialist Republics (U.S.S.R.) is a prime example of what happens to goods, services, and income for the majority of people. Russians waited in line for hours to receive "free" government handouts: soup, bread, shoes with paper soles, toilet paper, or medical care.

With complete federal control of healthcare, one can anticipate long wait lines for care by a small number of doctors the same way people in the U.S.S.R. had to wait for government handouts of bread and soup.

With inadequate facilities to provide timely care for patients, death-by-queueing would become a daily event. Innovation of new treatments would be a thing of the past.

For those who think the U.S.S.R. is not a good analogy, note the shortages of doctors, operating rooms, and burn units in government-controlled healthcare systems in Canada and Great Britain.[14]

One problem that remains is the lack of portability of health insurance. One hundred eighty million Americans have employer-supported health coverage. When they lose a job or change jobs, insurance coverage is also lost and care becomes unavailable. HIPAA (Health Insurance Portability and Accountability Act of 1996) was supposed to fix this: note the *P* in the title. It never did.

With market-based medicine, both insurance and, more important, access to care are completely portable. Patients hold insurance policies in their names, not through employers. The money to pay for care is in an HSA that the patient controls, not a third party or government.

Safety net

Market-based medicine will produce timely, high-quality health care at the lowest price for most Americans. However, there will be some who simply cannot get the care they need to survive, whether because of disability, severe illness or injury, or insufficient income. Most states would choose to develop a safety net for these individuals.

The construction of medical safety nets is best done at the local level. States know the residents, their needs, the local conditions (Rhode Island versus Montana, both with the same population size), and the resources available to serve their people.

The state should decide the qualification criteria for inclusion in their safety net rather than use a federally mandated, one-size-fits-all list. Insurance benefits would be decided by market forces, that is, by consumers, not by state or federal bureaucrats.

Two options immediately come to mind for the safety net: a high-risk pool and a state-funded HSA. States would be free to create whatever form of safety net they believe would work best.

High-risk pool

Before the ACA was passed, most states had what were called "high-risk pools." The risk was financial, not medical. These pools might be called high-expense pools, or support for the severely ill.

These pools consisted of individuals who could not obtain insurance at all or at an affordable price. The patients suffered from chronic renal, cardiac, or lung disease, diabetes with complications, cancer, or debilitating/degenerative diseases. Their care was exceedingly expensive, requiring teams of specialists to provide and coordinate their care as well as medications costing thousands of dollars per month.

Prior to 2010 and the ACA, the New Mexico High Risk Pool had 10,000 people enrolled and spent more than $200 million on their care annually.

High-risk pools set aside a large amount of money to pay for patient care. For-profit insurance companies are not involved. The costs of care for persons in high-risk pools are not included in the actuarial calculation of insurance premiums for the general population.

When the ACA mandated coverage of pre-existing conditions, the high-risk (high-cost) individuals had to be included in actuarial projections by insurance companies. This change, along with federal expansion of insurance benefits, caused insurance costs to skyrocket for everyone.

Restoration of high-risk pools would dramatically reduce insurance costs for the majority. In the market-based system with large family HSAs, the cost of a high-deductible catastrophic insurance would be surprisingly low, probably less than $400 per month if market forces are allowed to function.

HSA for impoverished

The high-risk pool concept won't work for healthy individuals whose difficulty paying for care is because of poverty, not high medical costs. States might choose to develop a safety net for these individuals.

Prior to the Great Depression, charitable organizations provided care for the indigent, the impoverished.[15] It was often spotty, sometimes inadequate, and generally unpredictable, and people died who might have been saved. Some form of structured safety net for the healthy-but-poor seems reasonable.

The HSA model can work as a safety net. The calculations that follow are based on demographic and financial data from Texas. However, this concept could be applied anywhere.

Just like the majority, safety net persons could have HSAs, from which they pay for care and purchase insurance. However, the state could contribute to their HSAs. There would still be a mandatory individual contribution; thus, consumers would still have *skin in the game.*

For this example, a time limit of six years of support was arbitrarily chosen. The person or family would contribute a small amount into the HSA and the state would match their contribution with a multiplier factor to leverage the amount into a sizeable HSA. The multiplication factor could decline over the years for adults. Contributions would continue for children at an 8-to-1 factor until the children reached 19 years of age, when contributions would cease.

Table 6-2 is an example of how this scheme would function with a family of four—two adults and two children—who would contribute $500 per adult and $250 per child into their HSA each year. The state contributes large but declining amounts over time. During the year, the family pays from their HSA for routine and urgent care below the high-deductible level of their insurance, say $10,000, at an estimated cost of $5000 per year paid from the HSA.

The amount remaining in the family HSA at year-end will be less than shown in the right column of Table 6-2. However, maximum out-of-pocket spending will be $10,000: $18,166 less than the average family had to spend in 2018. In fact, $10,000 is roughly what the average family expended on co-pays and deductibles *after* they gave $18,000 to insurance companies.

The HSA safety net in market-based medicine remains true to the foundational principles. People have numerous choices and can decide their care. Incentives are aligned rather than perverse. When consumers economize, both insurers and the state also save money. Dollar efficiency

Table 6-2: HSA Funds for Family of Four with Safety Net

Yr.	Multiplier		Family contrib.	State contrib.	Total HSA	HSA after insur-ance*
	Adult	Child				
1	18 to 1	8 to 1	$1,500	$22,000	$23,500	$18,500
2	18 to 1	8 to 1	$1,500	$22,000	$40,500	$35,500
3	14 to 1	8 to 1	$1,500	$18,000	$53,500	$48,500
4	14 to 1	8 to 1	$1,500	$18,000	$66,500	$61,500
5	10 to 1	8 to 1	$1,500	$14,000	$75,500	$70,500
6	10 to 1	8 to 1	$1,500	$14,000	$84,500	$79,500
7**	None	8 to 1	$1,500	$4,000	$85,000	$80,000

Contrib=contribution. (*) = The cost of high-deductible family insurance is assumed to be $10,000 per year. The volume of funds in "HSA after insurance" will be less than listed above by the amount expended for care during the year. (**) In year 7, support for adults ceases but continues for children until they are 19 years of age.

increases from the current 60 percent to well over 95 percent, as there is very little bureaucratic cost.

Most important, Americans retain their right to choose. They are personally responsible—they are not entitled. Entitlement is the death knell of freedom.

How much will the safety net cost taxpayers?

In February 2017, I testified before the Texas state legislature. I had given hundreds of lectures and speeches in the past, before medical audiences. This was my first foray into the world of politics. Though I was probably the oldest person in the chamber, I was nervous.

After my adequate but hardly stellar performance, one of the legislators approached me and asked to speak privately. I thought she was going to castigate me for doing a terrible job. Not so.

She wanted me to evaluate Texas's medical safety net, Medicaid, with respect to both adequacy of care and financial performance. Relieved that I hadn't messed up my testimony, I readily agreed.

The result was a series of articles and a monograph titled "The Saga of 1115–A Waiver Can Fix Texas Medicaid But Only Temporarily."[16] It confirmed the legislator's worst fears. Texas's medical safety net, supposedly administered by Texas, was actually controlled by federal mandates. Texas state spending on Medicaid, the largest expense item in the budget, was controlled by Washington and was consuming resources that Texas needed to expend on other priorities.

After reading my white paper, the legislator called me and asked if the only solution for Texas was what I had written, a waiver, which was a partial fix and temporary at that. "What could we do to fix our medical safety net permanently?" she queried. I answered honestly, "I don't know." I did not have an answer then. I do now: a market-based safety net.

Table 6-3: Comparing Medicaid and Market-Based Safety Net (MBSN)

	California	Texas
State population	39.9 mil	28.7 mil
Medicaid enrollment	13 mil	4.1 mil
Medicaid spending	$83 bil*	$30.6 bil
Savings with MBSN compared to Medicaid		
Years 1 & 2	$11.5 bil	$8.0 bil
Years 3 & 4	$24.5 bil	$12.1 bil
Years 5 & 6	$37.5 bil	$16.2 bil

mil=million. bil=billion. (*) California Medicaid spending data is from 2017; other data is based on 2018. pp=per person. Calculations assume no change in state Medicaid budget or enrollment.

Table 6-3 contrasts the financial effects of such an approach to the current Medicaid system, using the two most populous states: California, which expanded Medicaid under the ACA; and Texas, which did not. In California, 33 percent of the population is enrolled in Medicaid and in Texas, 14.3 percent. California spent an average of $6385 per enrollee while Texas spent $7463 per enrollee.

Based on the market-based safety net above and assuming no change in Medicaid enrollment or spending, California and Texas would save $8 billion and $11.5 billion, respectively, in years 1 and 2. In subsequent years, there are greater savings, as shown in figure 6-7.

The actual savings a state will experience depends on two factors: enrollment criteria and number of permanently disabled.

The main factor that affects spending by a safety net is caseload, the number of people enrolled. In turn, the enrollment criteria are decided by the state. When a state chooses market-based healthcare, the costs of the safety net will be much less than for the states that choose a government-controlled healthcare.

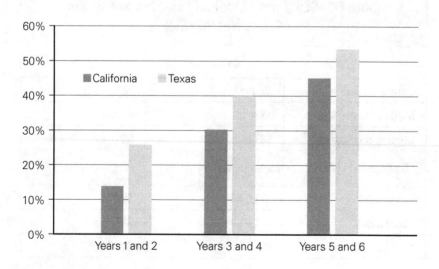

Figure 6-7: Savings with Market-Based Safety Net Compared to Medicaid

With Medicaid as the current safety net, fewer than 70 percent of U.S. physicians, nationally, accept new Medicaid-covered patients. In states like Texas, fewer than half of the doctors are willing to care for them. As a result, Medicaid (safety net) patients do not have adequate access to care.

Designers of medical safety nets must always keep in mind that a reduction in state spending is *not* the top priority. Job #1 is timely access to needed care for enrollees.

With market-based medicine, a physician does not know *or care* whether a patient is part of the safety net. Funds in the patient's HSA could come from his bank account or from the state. The physician is paid the same either way, with no insurance hassle. Patients will have access to timely care.

That's it!

With market-based medicine, the patient is in charge and chooses the doctor. The patient shops for the best price and pays the bill. The patient decides what insurance policy to purchase. Care providers are paid more. Market-based medicine is simple, user-friendly, and cheaper for taxpayers.

It was described here in fewer than 6000 words, in contrast to the 10,515,000 words of the first round of ACA regulations recorded in the Federal Register. Following is a list of activities missing from market-based medicine. I doubt *you* will miss them.

- Pre-authorization process
- Eligibility forms
- Verification procedure
- Approval/disapproval of care decisions
- Advanced premium tax credits
- Market stabilization payments (subsidies) to insurance companies
- Delay of care

- Denial of care
- Limited list of available doctors
- Long wait times (queueing)
- Pre-determined payment (reimbursement) schedule
- Discount-from-charges
- Billing and coding procedures
- Regulatory compliance
- Multiple reviews before payment
- All the costs in money and time associated with federal control and third-party payment systems.

Taxpayers no longer pay salaries to healthcare bureaucrats, namely, accountants, actuaries, administrators, agents, billers and coders, bureaucrats, compliance officers, consultants, in-person assisters, lawyers, middlemen, navigators, regulators, reviewers, rule writers, and the like.

Is market-based medicine for everyone? Yes and no. Yes, I believe it will work for all Americans. No, a healthcare system should not be imposed on anyone. With StatesCare, people in their states decide their healthcare. If some want Obamacare, some want single payer, and others want market-based medicine, they all have their choices.

Elevator pitch for market-based medicine

Management experts challenge someone with a new idea to pitch it in the time it takes an elevator to go from the first to the tenth floor, that is, less than a minute. This is called the "elevator pitch." Here is my elevator pitch for market-based medicine in 66 words, or about 30 seconds:

With market-based medicine, the patient chooses the caregiver, decides the care, agrees to the price, pays the bill, and evaluates the result. Insurance carriers and care providers compete for the patient's business. Neither government nor insurance has any say in medical decisions. Market-based medicine with a safety net offers the best balance of free-market dollar efficiency with society's need to protect the medically vulnerable.

Chapter Notes

1. The full text of the Tenth Amendment is as follows: "The powers not delegated to the United States by the Constitution, nor prohibited by it to the states, are reserved to the states respectively, or to the people."

2. See my article "A Doctor's Straight Talk: America, Your Health Care Is Not a Federal Responsibility" in *FoxNews.com*, Jan. 4, 2017.

3. There are numerous articles proposing and explaining *StatesCare* in *Fox News*, *The Hill*, the *Washington Examiner*, *NewzGroup*, the *Daily Caller*, and *RealClear Health*. I may or may not be the first to propose it, but I am probably the loudest.

4. See report by Tullis in the references.

5. Gruber, a Harvard professor, is famous (infamous?) for stating in public that "stupidity of the American voter" helped get the ACA enacted in to law.

6. See Staff in the references.

7. Busse amd Blümel's 2014 article "Germany: Health System Review" offers a good overview of the principles, structure, and history of federalized healthcare in Germany.

8. In 1974, Stephen Kerr wrote a seminal article in *Harvard Business Review* titled "On the Folly of Rewarding A While Hoping for B." This is a must-read!

9. Milliman Medical Index projects the average U.S. family of four will spend more than $28,166 in total healthcare expenses in 2018.

10. The Affordable Care Act included the Independent Payment Advisory Board (IPAB), which would meet in secret and decide which medical treatments the government would pay for and which they would not. The decisions would be based on what the panel decided was cost effective. The IPAB was so hated that it was repealed in 2018 by a Democrat-dominated House of Representatives.

11. Of the $28,166 expended by the average American family on healthcare in 2018, more than $18,000 was paid for insurance premiums and the remainder went to co-pays and deductibles.

12. There is a whole chapter titled "BARRC is Washington's Bite," in my book *The Cancer in the American Healthcare System*. This is painful but necessary reading.

13. A Hunter College researcher, Steffie Woolhandler, calculated the cost of federal bureaucracy as 31 percent of U.S. healthcare spending. This study was reported in 1999, long before the ACA. My own calculations, reported in 2010 in "Uproot U.S. Healthcare," suggested 40 percent was spent on BARRC, not care. With the cost of the ACA added, I fear that 50 percent of healthcare spending is wasted or dollar inefficient. However, assuming Woolhandler's 20-year-old

data is applicable today, 31 percent of the $3.5 trillion we spent on healthcare in 2018 means $1,085,000,000,000 *healthcare* dollars produced *no health CARE*.

14. For the evidence of what is called death-by-queueing, read my e-book *Single Payer Won't Save Us*, as well as my 2013 article "Cutting Healthcare Costs by Killing Patients" in *American Thinker*.

15. Another book well worth reading is Marvin Olasky's *The Tragedy of American Compassion*. This analysis of Medicare-for-All can be found at https://www.texaspolicy.com/right-on-healthcare-effect-on-patient-care-of-h-r-1384-medicare-for-all.

16. This paper can be found at: https://www.texaspolicy.com/right-on-healthcare-effect-on-patient-care-of-h-r-1384-medicare-for-all.

CHAPTER 7
Questions & Answers

A new healthcare system is bound to raise concerns. Here are questions that I have been asked followed by my best answers.

Question (Q): Isn't your market-based HSA just like what is now called an FSA?

Answer (A): FSA stands for "flexible savings account," which is a medical-use-only bank account in which employees and sometimes employers contribute pre-tax dollars. Unlike market-based HSAs, today's FSA has an upper limit for contributions; you must use-it-or-lose-it within one year; and the employer, not the patient, defines what is "medical use."

Q: With your free-market, profit-driven plan, won't poor people be left to die in the streets?

A₁: With the market-based approach, poor people can be covered by a safety net as the state decides. They could have large HSAs and high-deductible insurance just like everyone else. Providers will readily accept them into their medical or surgical practices because they are cash patients. They won't be dying in the streets.

A₂: Second, the people today who are "dying in the streets" generally have government insurance. Earlier in this book I described Americans experiencing death-by-queueing in Illinois, Maryland, and the VA system.[1]

A_3: The main beneficiaries of profit in market-based medicine are the patients, followed closely by the providers. Patients get control of their money and will be able to spend less. Doctors whose patients do well will be rewarded with profit. Even insurance companies will profit; moreover, with market-based medicine, insurance companies profit when patients do well both medically and financially.

Q: What happens when enrollees run out of money?

A_1: With market-based medicine, children and disabled and/or aged adults will never run out of money, because the state will continue its support indefinitely, as it does now. For able-bodied adults, state support ceases after six years, and at that time, patients are responsible for themselves and should be self-reliant.

A_2: If a state chose market-based medicine, some of the people who are not eligible for Medicaid might choose to contribute insufficient funds into their HSAs or not contribute at all, or not purchase insurance. They would then be responsible for their medical bills. If necessary, they would file for bankruptcy. The freedom to choose comes with the obligation to accept the consequences.

Q: Will market-based medicine work for the general, non-Medicaid population?

A: Market-based medicine was designed on principles, not for a specific population. It will work for anyone. If states want to adopt market-based medicine, it will work, but only if the states' residents want it. No system should be imposed on them.

Q: What happens to Medicare with StatesCare and market-based medicine?

A: The CBO has projected that Medicare will go broke—become insolvent—within seven years. At that time, Medicare will not be able to pay for hospital care for seniors. Something must be dome.

My own personal recommendation is to dissolve a Medicare program that has very obviously failed (or will fail in 2026). Stop contributions. Then, over a five-year period, pay out all the money that Americans have put into the trust and place that money into individual HSAs. Then let seniors control their own money the same way everyone else does in market-based medicine.

Q: What happens to CHIP with market-based medicine?

A: The Children's Health Insurance Program (CHIP) is a jointly funded, state–federal program to provide health insurance coverage for children in impoverished families whose incomes are above the threshold for Medicaid and less than 200 to 300 percent of the federal poverty level, depending on the state.

CHIP is different from Medicaid with respect to eligibility. Washington's CHIP contributions to states are higher than for Medicaid. CHIP has an element of personal responsibility—cost-sharing by the family—that is not present in Medicaid. CHIP is less expensive than Medicaid—$156 per child, per month—while Medicaid expends $237 per child, per month.

With market-based medicine, the state will determine eligibility for enrollment. If the standards chosen *do not* include the children currently in CHIP, there will be no change in that program. If the new standards *do* include the children currently in CHIP, they will be folded into the market plan and the amount of the block grant will need to be adjusted upwards to compensate.

Q: Why would insurance carriers sell your new "insurance" where *consumers* decide prices, replacing current policies where *insurers* decide how much they pay?

A: Because insurance companies are in business to sell policies.

In the current system, government rules dictate what policies insurance carriers can sell and for how much. In market-based healthcare, consumers can decide what to buy and at what price. Watch how this might play out.

A patient needs a hip replacement. The patient shops around and finds several doctors with good results, all of whom charge $20,000 for the procedure. The only difference is the type of insurance the doctors accept.

If the patient chooses a doctor who accepts new insurance, the patient will pay $10,000 to the doctor from his HSA, and insurance will pay the remaining $10,000. Thus, the doctor receives the agreed-upon price of $20,000.

If a patient chooses a doctor who contracts with a company who uses insurance currently in use, the insurance company pays the doctor a predetermined, contracted amount of, say, $12,000. Net cost to the patient is the same as with new insurance, $10,000. However, this is paid to insurance, not to the doctor. Net cost to the insurance company is $12,000 minus $10,000 (from patient's HSA), that is, $2000.

In a market-based environment, doctors would be free to choose insurance companies with whom to contract and insurance can offer whatever policies they believe will sell. Doctors would refuse to contract with old-style insurance, as they would be paid $8000 less. Insurance companies could not sell old-style insurance policies, as there would be no contracted physicians. Free-market conditions would force insurance companies to sell what consumers and physicians want, not what government dictates.

Q: Would doctors and hospitals agree to compete with each other? They certainly won't want to. Don't we need the government to force them to compete?

A₁: Keep in mind that government mandates in healthcare got us into this mess in the first place. No, we don't want or need federal or state government to enforce competition. The market will take care of those who refuse to give shoppers the information they need.

A₂: If a doctor or hospital refuses to provide the necessary data up front or provides confusing information, you know what will happen: consumers, spending their own money as they see fit, won't buy from the sellers who do not provide data they need in a form they can use. Will doctors willingly compete? Only the ones who want to stay in business. For my medical colleagues, don't forget that in a market-based system such as direct-pay, where government controls are absent, doctors will make more money, not less.

Q: If your idea is so good and obvious, why has no one done it before?

A: Government is always the one "fixing" healthcare. Yet government is the root cause of the problem. So every fix they enact makes healthcare worse, not better. Some providers have started free-market medical as well as surgical practices that have no government involvement. Both patients and doctors have found this no-government/no-insurance approach very much to their liking.

Q: What kind of preparation would be needed if a state chooses market-based medicine?

A: First, the state needs a global waiver of all federal mandates and a fixed-sum block grant, which will be negotiated between the state and Washington. Then, well in advance of a start date, there will be an extensive informational campaign presented to sellers—doctors, therapists, hospitals, pharmacies, insurance carriers, and others—about what consumers will expect from them, and to consumers about what their choices and responsibilities are. This is not a mandate in any way but merely advisory. The only mandates are the following: buyers (patients) must use their HSAs for medical costs only, and they are encouraged but not required to purchase high-deductible insurance. For sellers, one mandate might be a penalty for false advertising. That would be up to the state.

Q: Won't this be too big a shock to the country and the people?

A: Market-based medicine certainly will be a big change for everyone. Doctors and insurers would suddenly have to function in a free-market setting, which they have not done for more than eighty years. For consumers, it would be a smaller change, as they now function in a free market for everything except healthcare and education. For federal legislators, *StatesCare* would be a bitter pill: they would have to cede power (control) to the people in their states. For state legislators, the freedom from Washington will be both scary and invigorating.

All shocks can be scary: *different* is always frightening. Not all shocks are bad. If you get a big, unexpected raise in your paycheck, it is a shock, you are excited and happy, yet you are scared you won't get another one.

Q: How can you be so sure that market-based medicine will drive costs down?

A: It will drive costs down because market-based medicine has been proven in practice. Economics 101 teaches us that free-market forces produce the best balance of supply and demand, that you get the most product or service of the highest quality for the best price when buyers spend their own money and sellers compete for buyers' dollars. Look at the history of cell phones or Lasik surgery as examples of what happens when a product or service is exposed to free-market forces.

Q: A common aphorism is "If it sounds too good to be true, it *is*!!" Can you really get both better care and cheaper care?

A: This aphorism has been proven time and time again, yet, I stand by my assertion. Better and cheaper are possible in healthcare. With central economic planning, i.e., government control of healthcare, you can have *either* better *or* cheaper, but *never both*. In a free market, BOTH are available. Whether you are buying a car, having Lasik eye surgery, or getting a divorce online, better as well as cheaper can be found when sellers compete and buyers economize.

Q: Won't market-based medicine put a lot of people, possibly millions, out of work?

A: Yes, it will. The people who become unnecessary are healthcare administrators, bureaucrats, consultants, and lawyers whose salaries and benefits you have been paying for decades. Don't you want to stop wasting your "healthcare" dollars on them and spend your money on *patient care?*

Q: Why has the cost of healthcare in the United States become so completely unaffordable?

A₁: There are two reasons: one is value and the other is waste.

A₂: My grandfather graduated from the University of Pennsylvania Medical School in 1913. In his time, there were no clot-busting drugs; no heart surgery; no cures for any form of cancer; nor patients with "known" complex congenital heart diseases. So people with blood clots in their lungs, heart attacks, or cancer, or my babies (pediatric cardiology patients) with holes in their hearts, all died. Medical care was very inexpensive because doctors couldn't do much. There was very limited value available for the healthcare dollar because there was very little technology.

All the conditions mentioned above can now be treated. These treatments are expensive to create, to get FDA approval for, to produce, and to use. They are costly but valuable to patients because they save the lives of people who would otherwise die.

In 1960, before all the massive technological advances we enjoy today, the United States spent $147 per person on healthcare. In 2018, we will spend $10,526. That is a 7,061 percent increase in healthcare spending. Over the same period, net inflation was 727 percent for other spending.[2]

A₃: In my grandfather's day, there was no insurance as prepayment and no federal healthcare bureaucracy to speak of. The costs associated with third-party payment and government bureaucracy—now approaching half of all healthcare spending—simply did not exist.

Q: Healthcare is too complex for people to understand. They need guidance by the government.

A_1: The current system *is* too complex. And that complexity is unnecessary. Market-based medicine is simple. It works just like shopping for other goods or services, something people do every day.

A_2: "Guidance" is code for control.[3] Americans can either control themselves and be free, or accept government control and be dependent. There is really no in-between.

Chapter Notes

1. Illinois expanded its Medicaid program under Obamacare. As a result, many more people were insured. Sounds like a good outcome, but wait.

    . . . After the insurance companies were paid for the mandated benefits, there was too little money left over to pay the providers. Just like New Mexico, Illinois had to reduce its already low reimbursement schedule to doctors even further. This meant fewer providers would accept these low government payment schedules. The effect was to increase insurance coverage and decrease access to care. Bottom line, as reported by Nicholas Horton, "752 Illinoisans on the state's Medicaid waiting list have died awaiting needed care."

    -   The story of the needless death of a 12-year old boy in Maryland, Deamonte Driver, was described in Chapter 1.

    -   In 2015, the VA health system, our home-grown American single payer system, performed an *audit* to determine if veterans were receiving the medial care they needed. The auditors concluded that "47,000 veterans may have died" while waiting for approval to receive care.

    -   The effects of Medicaid expansion have been proven: enrollment increases, cost of insurance coverage goes up, and there are further cuts to payments to providers; so, as enrollment increases, access to care decreases. What I fail to comprehend is why people claim expansion is a good thing, and why so many states keep their expansion programs.

2. There numerous articles, charts, and infographics that describe healthcare spending in the U.S. over time. Two useful ones in the reference list are the article by Caitlin and Cowan and "U.S. National Health Expenditures as Percent of GDP from 1960 to 2019" on Statistica.com.

3. Every advisory, algorithm, counsel, direction, guideline, one-pager, opinion, and recommendation coming out of Washington has been turned into an enforceable commandment by hospital risk-management departments. The very last thing that healthcare needs or, more accurately, the last thing that *patients* need, is "guidance" from Washington.

Author's Evidence (References)

Before making any decision and especially before taking any action, one should have evidence. The assertions made in this book, the conclusions drawn, and the recommendations made are all based on proof. What follows is my evidence.

I provide all the evidence supporting my statements and conclusions, modeling the behavior our federal politicians should emulate but generally do not. They make statements and enact laws without proof-of-concept and evidence-of-effect (as engineers require). My evidence list includes nearly 500 references.

For those who want only the key readings, I have culled out the must-read references and list them first.

Key references

Ackoff, Russell. 1999. *Ackoff's Best: His Classic Writings on Management*. New York: Wiley & Sons.

Axelsson, Robert. 1998. "Toward an evidence-based health care management." *International Journal of Health Planning and Management* 13: 307-17.

Blahous, Charles. 2018. "The Costs of National Single-Payer Healthcare System." Mercatus Center, George Mason University.

Collins, Jim and Jeremy Porras. 1997. *Built to Last*. New York: HarperBusiness.

Forrester, Jay Wright. 1971. "The counterintuitive behavior of social systems." *Technology Review*, 73(3): 52-68.

Horton, Nicholas. 2016. "Hundreds on Medicaid waiting list in Illinois die while waiting for care." IllinoisPolicy.com.

Kaiser Family Foundation, 2009. "Health Care Costs—A Primer." Accessed at www. kff.org.

Kauffman, Draper. 1980. *Systems One: An Introduction to Systems Thinking*. Minneapolis: SA Carlton.

Kerr, Stephen. 1975. "On the folly of rewarding A While hoping for B." *Academy of Management Journal* 18: 769-783.

McSwane, J. David and Andrew Chavez. 2018. "A Preventable Tragedy," "Skimping on Care," "Texas pays billions for 'sham' networks," "Gloss-over of the Horror," and "Parents vs. the Austin machine (Part 5 of 5)." *Dallas Morning News*, June 3,4,5,6,7.

Olasky, Marvin. 1992. *The Tragedy of American Compassion*. Washington, D.C: Regnery Publishers.

Putkowski, Daniel. 2009. *Universal Coverage*. Media, PA: Hawser Press.

Rosenthal, Elizabeth. 2018. *An American Sickness – How Healthcare Became Big Business and How You Can Take It Back*. New York: Penguin Books.

Ruwart, Mary. 2018. *Death by Regulation*. Kalamazoo, MI: SunStar Press and Liberty International.

Waldman, Deane and Gavin McCullough. 2002. "A Calculus of *Unnecessary* Echocardiograms—Application of management principles to healthcare." *Pediatric Cardiology* 23: 186-191.

Waldman, Deane and Howard Lee Smith. 2007. "Thinking Systems Need Systems Thinking." *Systems Research and Behavioral Science* 24: 1-15.

Waldman, Deane. 2015. *The Cancer in the American Healthcare System – How Washington Controls and Destroys Our Health Care*. Corpus Christi: Strategic Book Publishing & Rights Agency.

Waldman, Deane. 2016. "Sovaldi is a bargain at $1000 a pill." *The Blaze*.

Waldman, Deane. 2017. "A doctor's straight talk: America, your health care is not a federal responsibility." *Fox News*.

Waldman, Deane. 2017. "California wants single payer and Texas wants free market — say hello to 'StatesCare.'" *The Hill*.

Woolhandler, Steffie, Terry Campbell, and David Himmelstein. 2003. "Costs of Health Care Administration in the United States and Canada." *New England Journal of Medicine* 349:768-775.

References

AAFP (American Academy of Family Physicians). 2018. "Direct Primary Care." *AAFP.com*.

Ackoff, Russell and Fred Emery. 1972. *On Purposeful Systems*. Chicago: Aldine-Atherton.

Ackoff, Russell. 1978. *The Art of Problem Solving, Accompanied by Ackoff's Fables*. New York: Wiley & sons.

Ackoff, Russell. 1989. "From Data to Wisdom." *Journal of Applied Systems Analysis* 16: 3-9.

Ackoff, Russell and Sheldon Rovin. 2003. *Redesigning Society*. Stanford, CA: Stanford Business Books.

ADHS (Arkansas Department of Human Services). 2018. "Arkansas Works."

Aiken, Linda, Sean Clarke, Douglas Sloane, Julie Sochalski and Jeffrey Silber. 2002. "Hospital Nurse Staffing and Patient Mortality, Nurse Burnout, and Job Dissatisfaction." *Journal of the American Medical Association* 286(16): 1987-1993.

Alexander, Jeffrey and M. Fennell. 1986. "Patterns of decision making in multihospital systems." *Journal of Health and Social Behavior,* 27(1): 14-27.

Alexander, Jeffrey, Richard Lichtenstein, Hyun Joo Oh, and Esther Ullman. 1998. "A causal model of voluntary turnover among nursing personnel in long-term psychiatric settings." *Research in Nursing and Health* 21(5): 415-427.

Allen, Stephen, Kimberlee Gauvreau, Barry Bloom, and Kathy Jenkins. 2003. "Evidence-based referral results in significantly reduced mortality after congenital heart surgery." *Pediatrics* 112(1): 24-28.

Amadeo, Kimberly. 2017. "How much did Obamacare cost?" *The Balance*.

Andrews, Kate. 2015. "Universal healthcare and market-based systems aren't mutually exclusive." *Adamsmith.org,* April 21.

Angell, Marcia. 2002. "Forgotten domestic crisis." *New York Times*.

Anonymous. 2003. "Research Notes." *Healthcare Executive* 18(2): 42.

Anonymous. 2004. "Hospital CEO turnover remains stable in 2003." *Healthcare Executive* 19(4): 65.

Antonisse, Larisa and Rachel Garfield. 2018. "The Relationship Between Work and Health: Findings from a Literature Review." Kaiser Family Foundation.

"America's Health Future." 2018. Interview with CMS Administrator Seema Verma. *Washington Post*.

Archambault, Joshua. 2013. "Will ACA Cause Rate Shock in Massachusetts? It Appears So, Small Biz to See Premiums Rise Up to 97%." *Pioneerinstitute.org.*

Argote, Linda and Dennis Epple. 1990. "Learning Curves in Manufacturing." *Science,* 247: 920–24.

Aronson, Daniel. 1998. "Overview of Systems Thinking." www. thinking.net. Accessed Feb 2004.

Arndt, Margaret and Barbara Bigelow. 2000. "The transfer of business practices into hospitals: history and implications." *Advances in Health Care Management* Vol. 1: 339-368.

Ashmos, Donde and Reuben McDaniel, Jr. 1991. "Physician participation in hospital strategic decision making: The effect of hospital strategy and decision content." *Health Services Research* 26(3): 375-401.

Ashmos, Donde and Reuben McDaniel, Jr. 1996. "Understanding the participation of critical task specialists in strategic decision making." *Decision Science* Winter 27(1): 103-121.

Ashmos, Donde, Dennis Duchon, and Reuben McDaniel, Jr. 1998. "Participation in strategic decision making: The role of organizational predisposition and issue interpretation." *Decision Science* 29(1): 25-51.

Ashmos, Donde, Joseph Huonker, and Reuben McDaniel, Jr. 1998. "The effect of clinical professional and middle manager participation on hospital performance. *Health Care Management Review* 23(4): 7-20.

Ashmos, Donde, Dennis Duchon, and Reuben McDaniel, Jr. 2000. "Organizational response to complexity: the effect on organizational performance." *Journal of Organizational Change* 13(6): 577- 594.

Associated Press. 2007. "Doctor contrasts his cancer care with uninsured patient who died."

Associated Press (London). 2016. "Battle Over Health Care: UK Doctors Walk Off the Job." April 26.

Associated Press. 2018. "Lawsuit filed over Arkansas Medicaid work requirement."

Atlas, Scott. 2009. "10 Surprising Facts about American Health Care." National Center for Policy Analysis.

Atwater, J. Brian and Paul Pittman. 2006. "Facilitating systemic thinking in business classes." *Decision Sciences Journal of Innovative Education.* 4(2): 273-292.

Baiker, Katherine, Sarah Taubman, Heidi Allen, Mira Bernstein, et al. 2013. "The Oregon Experiment—Effects of Medicaid on clinical outcomes." *New England Journal of Medicine,* 368;18: 1713-22.

Baker, Edward. 2001. "Learning from the Bristol Inquiry." *Cardiology in the Young* 11: 585-587.

Baker, Ted. 1999. *Doing Well By Doing Good*. Economic Policy Institute, Washington, DC.

Baloff, Nicholas. 1971. "Extension of the Learning Curve—Some Empirical Results." *Operational Research Quarterly* 1971; 22(4): 329–40.

Barzansky, Barbara and Sylvia Etzel. 2001. "Educational programs in the US medical schools 2000-2001." *Journal of American Medical Association* 286(9): 1049-1055

Barron, John and Stephen McCafferty. 1977. "Job search, labor supply, and the quit decision: Theory and evidence." *American Economic Review* 67(4): 683-691.

Bates, David, Deborah Boyle, Martha Vander Vliet, James Schneider, and Lucian Leape. 1995. "Relationship between medication errors and adverse drug events." *Journal of General Internal Medicine* 10(4) 199-205,

"BCCS (Breast and Cervical Cancer Support) Eligibility." *Texas Health and Human Services.*

Becker, Thomas. 2004. "Why pragmatism is not practical." *Journal of Management Inquiry September* 13(3): 224-230.

Beedham, Thomas. 1996. "Why do young doctors leave medicine?" *British Journal of Hospital Medicine* 55(11): 699-701. Editorial Comments by Elizabeth Paice 1997; 90(8): 417-418 and by John Davis 1997; 90(10): 585.

Beinhocker, Eric. 1997. "Strategy at the edge of chaos". *The McKinsey Quarterly* Winter #1, pp. 24-40.

Beller, George. 2000. "Academic Health Centers: The making of a crisis and potential remedies." *Journal of the American College of Cardiology* 36:1428-31.

Bender, Claire, Susan DeVogel, and Robert Blomberg. 1999. "The socialization of newly hired medical staff into a large health system." *Health Care Management Review* 24:95-108.

Benson, Guy. 2018. "Single-Payer in Crisis: Britain's NHS Cancels 50,000 Surgeries Amid Long Waits for Care, 'Third World' Conditions." *Townhall.com.* January 5.

Berenson, Robert, Paul Ginsburg, and Jessica May. 2007. "Hospital-physician relations: Cooperation, competition, or separation?" *Health Affairs* 26(1): w31-w43.

Berger, J.E. and R.L. Boyle RL. 1992. "How to avoid the high costs of physician turnover." *MGM Journal* pp. 80-91.

Berry, LL. 2004. "The Collaborative Organization: Leadership lessons from Mayo Clinic." *Organizational Dynamics* 33(3): 228-242.

Berta, Whitney and G. Ross Baker. 2004. "Factors that impact the transfer and retention of best practices for reducing error in hospital." *Health Care Management Review* 29(2): 90-97.

(von) Bertalanffy, Ludwig. 1968, revised 1976. *General System theory: Foundation, development, applications.* New York: George Braziller.

Berwick, Donald. 1989. "Continuous Improvement as an ideal in health care." *New England Journal of Medicine* 320(1): 53-56.

Berwick, Donald, A. Blanton Godfrey, and Jane Roessner. 1990. *Curing Health Care.* San Francisco: Jossey-Bass.

Bettis, Richard and C.K. Prahahald. 1995. "The dominant logic: retrospective and extension." *Strategic Management Journal* 16(1): 237-252.

Birkmeyer, John, Samuel Finlayson, Anna Tosteson, Sandra Sharp, Andrew Warshaw, and Elliot Fisher. 1999. "Effect of Hospital Volume on In-hospital Mortality with Pancreaticoduodenectomy." *Surgery* 125: 250–56

Birkmeyer, John, Therese Stukel, Andrea Siewers, and Philip Goodney. 2003. "Surgeon volume and operative mortality in the United States." *New England Journal of Medicine* 349: 2117-27.

Bisognano, Maureen. 2004. "What Juran says. One of four essays on "Can the gurus' concepts cure healthcare?" In *Quality Progress* September pp. 33-34.

Blackburn, Richard and Benson Rosen. 1993. "Total quality and human resource management: lessons learned from Baldrige award-winning companies." *Academy of Management Executive* 7: 49-66.

Bloom, Joan, Jeffrey Alexander, and Beverly Nuchols. 1992. "The effect of the social organization of work on the voluntary turnover rate of hospital nurses in the United States." *Social Science and Medicine* 34(12): 1413-1424.

Blumenthal, David and William Hsiao. 2005. "Privatization and Its Discontents-The Evolving Chinese Health Care System." *New England Journal of Medicine* 353: 1165-1170.

Bodkin, Henry. 2016. "Children's healthcare at 'breaking point', warn doctors." *Telegraph/U.K.*, August 16.

Boffey, Daniel and Denis Campbell. 2014. "David Cameron warned NHS in danger of collapse within 6 years." *The Observer*, June 28.

Bole, Thomas and W.B. Bondeson. 1991. *Rights to Health Care.* London: Kluwer Academic Publishers.

Bonacich, Phillip. 1987. "Power and Centrality: A Family of Measures." *American Journal of Sociology* 92(5): 1170-82.

Borda, Robert and Ian Norman. 1997. "Factors influencing turnover and absence of nurses: a research review." *International Journal of Nursing Studies* 34(6): 385-394.

Boyd, Dan. 2016. "NM faces $417M Medicaid shortfall." *Albuquerque Journal*, A16.

Brady, Rep. Kevin. 2010. "Obamacare Complicated? Check Out the Flow Chart." *The Daily Bail*.

Bragg, J.E. and R. Andrews. 1973. "Participative decision-making: An experimental study in a hospital." *Journal of Applied Behavioral Science* 9: 727-735.

Brass, Daniel. 1984. "Being in the right place: A structural analysis of individual influence in an organization." *Administrative Science Quarterly*, 29: 518-539.

Brass, Daniel and Marlene Burkhardt. 1993. "Potential power and power use: An investigation of structure and behavior." *Academy of Management Journal* 36(3): 441-470.

Brennan, Troyen, A.R. Localio, Lucian Leape, N.M. Laird, L. Peterson, H.H. Hiatt, and B.A. Barnes. 1990. "Identification of Adverse Effects Occurring during Hospitalization: A Cross-Sectional Study of Litigation, Quality Assurance, and Medical Records at Two Teaching Hospitals." *Annals of Internal Medicine* 112: 221-226.

Brennan, Troyen, Colin Sox, and Helen Burstin. 1996. "Relation Between Negligent Adverse Events and the Outcomes of Medical-Malpractice Litigation." *New England Journal of Medicine* 335:1963-1967.

Brian. 2004. "NHS Revolution: nurses to train as surgeons." *The Independent* (London), December 6.

Brook, Robert and Kathleen Lohr. 1987. "Monitoring quality of care in the Medicare Program." *Journal of the American Medical Association* 258: 3138-3141.

Brockschmidt, FR. 1996. "Corporate culture: does it play a role in health care management?" *Certified Registered Nurse Anesthetist* 1994; 5:93-6.

Broder, D.S. 2001. "Need for capable government has never been clearer." *Albuquerque Journal*, October 21.

Broder, D.S. 2002. "Health cost spike can't be ignored." *Albuquerque Journal*, April 17.

Broder, D.S. 2005. "Unfunded mandates still plaguing states, cities." *Albuquerque Journal*, March 18.

Brooks, Ian. 1996. "Using rituals to reduce barriers between sub-cultures." *Journal of Management in Medicine* 10(3): 23-30.

Brotherton, Sarah. 2001. "U.S. Graduate medical education, 2000-2001." *Journal of American Medical Association* 286(9): 1056-1060.

Bryson, R.W., M. Aderman, J.M. Sampiere, L. Rockmore, and T. Matsuda. 1985. "Intensive care nurse: Job tension and satisfaction as a function of experience level." *Critical Care Medicine* 13(9): 767-769.

Buckbinder, Sharon, Modena Wilson, Clifford Melick, and Nel Powe. 2001. "Primary care physician job satisfaction and turnover." *American Journal of Managed Care* 7(7): 701-713.

Bullard, Ben. 2013. "Report: 70 Percent of California Doctors Won't Participate in Obamacare." *Personalliberty.com*.

Burt, Ronald and Michael Miner. 1983. *Applied Network Analysis: A Methodological Introduction.* Beverly Hills: Sage.

Busse, Reinhard and Miriam Blümel. 2014. "Germany: Health System Review." *Health Systems in Transition* 16(2): 1-296.

Butterworth, P, Liana Leach, Lyndall Strazdina, and Sarah Olesen. 2011. "The psychosocial quality of work determines whether employment has benefits for mental health: results from a longitudinal national household panel survey." *Occupational and Environmental Medicine* 68(11): 806-812.

Cameron, Kim. 1991. "Cultural congruence, Strength, and Type: Relationships to Effectiveness." *Research in Organizational Change and Development* 5: 23-58.

Cannon, Michael. 2016. "Aetna Has Revealed Obamacare's Many Broken Promises." *Time.com*.

Carleson, Susan. 2012. "The Reagan Remedy for Medicaid." *American Thinker.com*

Carvel, John. 2005. "NHS cash crisis bars knee and hip replacements for obese." *Manchester Guardian*, November 23.

Catlin, Aaron and Cathy Cowan. 2015. "History of Health Spending in the United States, 1960-2013." *CMS.gov*.

Catron, David. 2013. "The Wheels Come Off Obamacare." *American Spectator*.

Cavanaugh, Stephen. 1990. "Predictors of Nursing staff turnover." *Journal of Advanced Nursing* 15(3): 373-380.

Champy, James. 1995. *Reengineering Management.* New York: HarperBusiness.

Chassin, Marc. 1998. "Is health care ready for six sigma quality?" *The Millbank Quarterly* Winter v76 i4 p 565(2).

Christenson, Clayton, Richard Bohmer, and John Kenagy. 2000. "Will disruptive innovations cure health care?" *Harvard Business Review* 78(5): 102-112.

Clark, Richard. 1996. "Outcome as a Function of Annual Coronary Artery Bypass Graft Volume." *Annals of Thoracic Surgery* 6(1):21–26.

Clinton, William. 1996. "Statement on Signing the Personal Responsibility and Work Opportunity Reconciliation Act of 1996." *The American Presidency Project*.

Cochrane, Archie. 1972. "Effectiveness and Efficiency: Random Reflections of Health Services." London: Nuffield Trust.

Coeling, Harriet and James Wilcox. 1988. "Understanding organizational culture: A key to management decision-making." *Journal of Nursing Administration* 18(11): 16-24.

Coeling, Harriet and Lillian Simms. 1993. "Facilitating Innovations at the Nursing Unit Level through Cultural Assessment, Part 1: How to keep Management Ideas from Falling on Deaf Ears." *Journal of Nursing Administration* 23: 46-53.

Coeling, Harriet and Lillian Simms. 1993. "Facilitating Innovation at the unit level through cultural assessment, Part 2." *Journal of Nursing Administration* 23(5): 13-20.

Cohn, Kenneth and Michael Peetz. 2003. "Surgeon frustration: Contemporary problems, practical solutions." *Contemporary Surgery.* 59(2): 76-85.

Cohn, Kenneth, Sandra Gill, and Richard Schwartz. 2005. "Gaining hospital administrators' attention: Ways to improve physician- hospital management dialogue." *Surgery* 137:132-140.

Cohn, Kenneth. 2005. "Embracing Complexity," from Cohn KH. *Better Communication for Better Care: Mastering Physician- Administrator Collaboration,* Chicago: Health Administration Press, Pp. 30-38.

Coleman, James, Elihu Katz E, and Herbert Menzel. 1957. "The diffusion of an innovation among physicians." *Sociometry* 20(4): 253-270.

Collins, Jim. 2001. *Good to Great.* New York: HarperBusiness.

Conger, Jay and Rabindra Kanungo. 1988. "The empowerment process: Integrating theory and practice." *Academy of Management Review* 13: 471-482.

Connelly, Lynne, Marge Bott, Nancy Hoffart, and Roma Lee Taunton. 1997. "Methodologic triangulation in a study of nurse retention." *Nursing Research* Sept/Oct 46(5): 299-302.

Consumer Reports. February 2007. "Get better care from your doctor."

Cooke, Robert and Janet Szumal. 1991. "Measuring normative beliefs and shared behavioral expectations in organizations: The Reliability and Validity of the Organizational Culture Inventory." *Psychological Reports* 72: 1299-1330.

Cotton, John, David Vollrath, Kirk Froggatt, and Mark Lengnick-Hall. 1988. "Employee participation: Diverse forms and different outcomes." *Academy of Management Review,* 13(1): 8-22.

Coulson, John, Rhea Seddon, and William Readdy. 2008. "Advancing Safety in pediatric cardiology—Approaches Developed in Aviation." *Congenital Cardiology Today,* Vol 6, No. 3, Pp 1-10.

Covey, Steven. 1989. *The Seven Habits of Highly Effective People.* New York: Simon & Schuster.

Cox, Archibald. 1987. *The Court and the Constitution.* Boston: Houghton Miflin.

Cubanski, Juliette, Tricia Neuman, and Meredith Freed. 2019. "The Facts on Medicare Spending and Financing." Kaiser Family Foundation.

D'Aunno, Thomas, J.A. Alexander JA, and C. Laughlin. 1996. "Business as usual? Changes in Health Care's workforce and organization of work." *Hospital and Health Services Administration* 16: 3-18.

Daschle, Tom, Jeanne Lambrew, and Scott Greenberger. 2008. *Critical: What We Can Do About the Health-Care Crisis.* New York: St. Martin's Press.

Davidson, Mark. 1983. *Uncommon Sense—The Life and Thought of Ludwig von Bertalanffy (1901-1972), Father of General Systems Theory.* Los Angeles: Tarcher.

Davies, Huw, Sandra Nutley, and Russell Mannion. 2000. "Organizational Culture and Quality of Health Care." *Quality in Health Care* 9: 111-9.

Davis, Karen, Cathy Schoen, and Kristof Stremikis. 2010. "Mirror, Mirror on the Wall: How the Performance of the U.S. Health Care System Compares Internationally, 2010 Update." The Commonwealth Fund.

De Jonge, Jan, Peter Janssen, J. de Jonge, and Arnold Bakker. 1999. "Specific determinants of intrinsic work motivation, burnout and turnover intentions: a study among nurses." *Journal of Advanced Nursing* 29(6): 1360-1369.

Deal, Terrence and Allan Kennedy. 1982. *Corporate Culture: Rites and Rituals of Corporate Life.* Cambridge, MA: Perseus Publishing.

Deal, Terrence and Allan Kennedy. 1999. *The New Corporate Cultures.* Reading, MA: Perseus Books.

Decker, Sandra. 2012. "In 2011 Nearly One-Third of Physicians Said They Would Not Accept New Medicaid Patients, But Rising Fees May Help." *Health Affairs* 31(8): 1673-79.

Diamond, Dan. 2013. "More Doctors Are Quitting Medicare. Is Obamacare Really to Blame?" *CaliforniaHealthline.com.*

Dilts, David and Alan Sandler. 2006. "The 'Invisible' Barriers to Clinical Trials: The impact of Structural, Infrastructural, and Procedural Barriers to Opening Oncology Clinical Trials." *Journal Clinical Oncology,* 24(28): 4545-52.

Dixon, K. 2004. "HMOs bringing back unpopular cost controls- Survey." *Reuters,* 8/10/04.

Donabedian, Avedis. 1985. *Explorations in Quality Monitoring and Assessment and Monitoring—Volume III, The Methods and Findings of Quality Assessment and Monitoring: An Illustrated Analysis.* Ann Arbor: Health Administration Press.

Douglas, C.H., A. Higgins, C. Dabbs, and M Walbank. 2004. "Health impact assessment for the sustainable futures of Salford." *Journal of Epidemiology and Community Health* 58: 642-648.

Drake, David, Susan Fitzgerald, and Mark Jaffe. 1993. *Hard Choices—Health Care at What Cost?* Kansas City: Andrews & McMeel.

Dwore, R.B. and B.P. Murray. 1989. "Turnover at the top: Utah hospital CEOs in a turbulent era." *Hospital Health Services Administration* Fall, 34(3): 333-351.

Editorial Board. 2018. "Why are drugs cheaper in Europe?" *Wall Street Journal*, October 28.

Edmondson, Amy. 1996. "Learning from mistakes is easier said than done: Group and organizational influences on the detection and correction of human error." *Journal of Applied Behavioral Science*, 32(1): 5-28.

Edmondson, Amy. 2008. "The Competitive Imperative of Learning." *Harvard Business Review* July-August: 60-67.

Edmonton TV. Opposition demand health care review. Accessed 3/11/11.

Ellis, Libby, Alison Canchola, David Spiegel, Uri Ladabaum, Robert Haile, and Scarlett Lin Gomez. 2017. "Trends in Cancer Survival by Health Insurance Status in California from 1997 to 2014." *JAMA Oncology* 4(3): 317-323.

Ellis, Stephen, William Weintraub, David Holmes, Richard Shaw, Peter Block, and Spencer King. 1997. "Relation of Operator Volume and Experience to Procedural Outcome of Percutaneous Coronary Revascularization at Hospitals with High Interventional Volumes." *Circulation* 95: 2479–84.

Engstrom, P. 1995. "Cultural differences can fray the knot after MDs, hospitals exchange vows." *Medical Network Strategy Report*, 4:1-5.

Epstein, Richard. 1999. *Mortal Peril—Our Inalienable Right to Health Care?* Cambridge, MA: Perseus Books.

Eubanks, P. 1991. "Identifying your hospital's corporate culture." *Hospitals* 65: 46.

Executive Order 13765. 2017. "Minimizing the Economic Burden of the Patient Protection and Affordable Care Act Pending Repeal." *The White House.*

Executive Order 13828. 2018. "Reducing Poverty in America by Promoting Opportunity and Economic mobility." *The White House.*

Fallin, Mary. March 5, 2018. "Executive Order 2018-05."

Feldstein, Paul. 2005. *Health Care Economics*, 6th ed. Clifton, N.Y.: Thomson Delmar Learning.

Fennell, Mary and Jeffrey Alexander. 1987. "Organization boundary spanning and institutionalized environments." *Academy of Management Journal* 30: 456-476.

Ferlie, Ewan, Louise Fitzgerald, and Martin Wood. 2000. "Getting evidence into clinical practice: an organizational behavior perspective." *Journal of Health Services Research & Policy* 5(2): 96-102.

Ferlie, Ewan and Stephen Shortell. 2001. "Improving the quality of health care in the United Kingdom and the United States: A framework for change." *Millbank Quarterly* 79(2): 281-315.

Ferrara-Love, R. 1997. "Changing organizational culture to implement organizational change." *Journal of Perianesthesia Nursing* 12: 12-6.

Finley, Allysia. 2018. "ObamaCare Is Robbing Medicaid's Sickest Patients." *Wall Street Journal*, July 25.

Fiol, C. Marlene, Edward O'Connor, and Herman Aguinis. 2001. "All for one and one for all? The development and transfer of power across organizational levels." *Academy of Management Review*, 26(2): 224-242.

Fitzgerald, F. Scott. 1936. *The Crack-Up*. New York: New Directions Books.

Fourcade, Martha and Natasha Rausch. 2017. "Humana to Cut 5.7% of Workforce Amid Uncertainty in Health Care." *Bloomberg.com*.

Franczyk, Annemarie. 2000. "Turnover in hospital CEOs brings change to healthcare industry." *Business First, Buffalo.* 12(44), pp. 1-2.

Freiberg, Kevin and Jackie Freiberg. 1996. *Nuts! Southwest Airlines' Crazy Recipe for Business and Personal Success*. New York: Broadway Books.

Friedman, Eric and Eli Adashi. 2010. "The right to health as the unheralded narrative of health care reform." *Journal of the American Medical Association* 304(23): 2639-2640.

Galloro, Vince. 2001. "Staffing outlook grim. High turnover expected to continue in skilled nursing, assisted living.". *Modern Healthcare* 31(8): 64.

Garson, Arthur. 2001. "The Edgar Mannheim Lecture: From white teeth to heart transplants: evolution in international concepts of the quality of healthcare." *Cardiology in the Young* 11: 601-608.

Gawande, Atul. 2007. "A Lifesaving checklist." *New York Times. com* December 30.

Gawande, Atul. 2011. "Can we lower medical costs by giving the neediest patients better care?" *New Yorker.* January 24.

Gawande, Atul. 2011. "Cowboys and Pit Crews." *The New Yorker*, May 26.

Gearey, Robyn. 2015. "Would Concierge Medicine Offer the Right Health Care for You?" *Dailyfinance.com*.

Gentry, W.D. and K.R. Parkes. 1982. "Psychologic stress in the ICU and non-intensive unit nursing: A review of the past decade." *Heart & Lung* 11(1): 43-47.

Gerowitz, M, L. Lemieux-Charles, C. Heginbothan, and B. Johnson. 1996. "Top Management Culture and Performance in Canadian, UK and US Hospitals." *Health Services Management Research* 6 (3): 69-78.

Gibson, Marcia, Hilary Thomson, Kasia Banas, Vittoria Lutje, Martin McKee, Susan Martin, Candida Fenton, Claire Bambra, and Lyndal Bond. 2018. "Welfare-to-work interventions and their effects on the mental and physical health of lone parents and their children." *Cochrane Database of Systematic Reviews* 2018(2).

Ginn, Vance and Deane Waldman. 2017. " The Senate's healthcare double whammy: fewer jobs and less care." *The Hill.*

Glaser, Susan, Sonia Zamanou, and Kenneth Hacker. 1987. "Measuring and Interpreting Organizational Culture." *Management Communication Quarterly* 1 (2): 173-98.

Goldenstein, Taylor. 2018. "Sendero Health Plans to withdraw from Medicaid, CHIP markets." *American Statesman.*

Goldman, Dana and Elizabeth McGlynn. 2005. "U.S. Health Care: Facts about Cost, Access and Quality." Rand Report CP484.1.

Goldratt, Eliyahu and Jeff Cox.1984. *The Goal–A Process of Ongoing Improvement.* Great Barrington, MA: North River Press.

Goldsmith, Jeff. 2003. *Digital Medicine: Implications for Healthcare Leaders.* Chicago: Health Administration Press.

Goldworth, Amnon. 2008. "Human rights and the right to health care." In: Weisstub, David and Guillermo Diaz Pintos, *Autonomy and Human Rights in Health Care.* The Netherlands: Springer.

Grant, Rebecca. 2016. "The U.S. Is Running Out of Nurses." *TheAtlantic.com.*

Gray, Alistair, V.L. Phillips, and Charles Normand. 1996. "The costs of nursing turnover: Evidence from the British National Health Service." *Health Policy* 38: 117-128.

Greco, Peter and John Eisenberg. 1993. "Changing Physicians' Practices." *New England Journal of Medicine* 329(17): 1271-1274.

Greene, J. 1995. "Clinical integration increases profitability, efficiency—study." *Modern Healthcare*, February p. 39.

Groupman, Jerome. 2007. *How Doctors Think.* New York: Houghton Miflin.

Grout, John. 2003. "Preventing medical errors by designing benign failures." *Joint Commission Journal on Quality and Safety* 29(7): 354-362.

Hadley, J., J.M. Mitchell, D.P. Sulmasy, and M.G. Bloch. 1999. "Perceived financial incentives, HMO market penetration, and physicians' practice styles and satisfaction." *Health Services Research* Apr 34(1 Pt 2): 307-321.

Haft, Harold. "The Right to Basic Health Care is Afforded to Every Citizen of the United States." *Physician Executive* Jan-Feb 2003.

Haislmaier, Edmund. 2015. "2014 Enrollment Increase Due Almost Entirely to Medicaid Expansion." *Heritage Foundation*.

Hale, Celia. 2003. "NHS Chiefs 'forced into trickery.'" *London Times*, May 7.

Hall, Edward and Mildred Reed Hall. 1990. *Understanding Cultural Differences*. Yarmouth, Maine: Intercultural Press.

Hammer, Michael and James Champy. 1994. *Reengineering the Corporation-A Manifesto for Business Revolution*. New York: HarperBusiness.

Hammer, Michael. 2001. *The Agenda*. New York: Crown Business.

Hannan, E.L., M. Racz, RE Kavey, J.M Quaegebeur, and R. Williams. 1998. "Pediatric Cardiac Surgery: The Effect of Hospital and Surgeon Volume on In-hospital Mortality." *Pediatrics* 101(6): 963-69.

Hariri, S., A.L. Prestipino, and H.E. Rubash. 2007. "The Hospital-Physician Relationship: Past, Present and Future." *Clinical Orthopaedics and Related Research* 457: 78-86.

Hart, Angela. 2018. "More undocumented immigrants would qualify for health care in $250 million California plan." *Sacramento Bee*.

Hart, L.G., D.G. Robertson, D.M. Lishner, and R.A. Rosenblatt. 1993. "CEO turnover in rural northwest hospitals." *Hospital Health Services Administration* Fall; 38(3): 353-374.

Haskins, Ron. Testimony before House of Representatives Ways and Means Committee, on Effects of the 1996 Welfare Reform Law, July 19, 2006.

Haskins, Ron. Testimony before House of Representatives Ways and Means Committee, on Challenging Facing Low-income Individuals and Families, February 11, 2015.

Hawkes, Nigel. 2002. "Patients get power to select surgeons." *London Times*, January 18.

Hayes, Tara O'Neill. 2017. "How Many Are Newly Insured as a Result of the ACA?" *American Action Forum*.

Henninger, Daniel. 2003. "Marcus Welby doesn't live here anymore." *Wall Street Journal*, January 10.

Herzlinger, Regina. 1997. *Market-Driven Health Care*. Reading MA: Addison-Wesley.

Herzlinger, Regina. 2003. "Back in the USSR." *Wall Street Journal*, November 26.

Heskett, James and W. Earl Sasser, and Leonard Schlesinger. *The Service Profit Chain*. New York: Free Press.

HHS REPORT: "Average Health Insurance Premiums Doubled Since 2013." May 2017.

Hill, Laurence and James Madara. 2005. "Role of the Urban Academic Medical Center in US Health Care." *JAMA* 294(17): 2219-2220.

Hilts, Philip. 1993. "Health-care Chiefs' pay rises at issue." *New York Times,* June 23.

Himmelstein, David, Elizabeth Warren, Deborah Thorne, and Steffie Woolhandler. 2005. "Illness and Injury as Contributors To Bankruptcy." *Health Affairs (Millwood)* Jan-Jun: Suppl Web Exclusives W5-63–W5-73.

Hint Health. 2017. "Direct Primary Care Trends Report 2017."

Hock, Dee. 1999. *Birth of the Chaordic Age.* San Francisco: CA: Berrett-Koehler.

Hogberg, David. 2013. "Why The 'Young Invincibles' Won't Participate In The ObamaCare Exchanges and Why It Matters." *NationalCenter.org.*

Horton, Nicholas. 2015. "Shocking report reveals rampant welfare fraud in Arkansas." *Townhall.com.*

Howard, Philip. 2002. "There is no 'right to sue.'" *Wall Street Journal,* July 31.

Hussey, Peter and Gerard Anderson. 2005. "Health spending in the United States and the rest of the industrialized world." The Commonwealth Fund.

Hyman, Mark. 2010. "Obesity in America: Are Factory Farms, Big Pharma and Big Food to Blame?" HuffingtonPost.com.

Iglehart, J. 1998. "Forum on the future of academic medicine: Session III—Getting from Here to There." *Academic Medicine* 73 (2): 146-151

Ingram, Jonathan. 2015. "Stop the scam — How to prevent welfare fraud in your state." Foundation for Government Accountability.

Irvine, Diane and Martin Evans. 1995. "Job satisfaction and Turnover among nurses: Integrating research findings across studies." *Nursing Research* July/August 44(4): 246-253.

Jacobs, Chris. 2013. "Morning Bell: Obamacare's Dirty Dozen Implementation Failures." *Heritage.org,* July 8.

Jain, K.K. 2005. "Personalised medicine for cancer: from drug development into clinical practice." *Expert Opinions in Pharmacotherapy* 6(9): 1463-1476.

Japsen, Bruce. 2012. "U.S. Workforce Illness Costs $576B Annually from Sick Days to Workers Compensation." *Forbes,* September 12.

Jenkins, Kathy, Kimberlee Gauvreau, Jane Newburger, Thomas Spray, James Moller, and Lisa Iezzoni. 2002. "Consensus- based method for risk adjustment for surgery for congenital heart disease." *Journal of Thoracic & Cardiovascular Surgery* January 123: 110-118.

Jha, Ashish, Jonathan Perlin, Kenneth Kizer, and R. Adams Dudley RA. 2003. "Effect of the transformation of the Veterans Affairs Health Care System and the quality of care." *New England Journal of Medicine* 348(2): 2218-2227.

Jiang, H. Joanna, Bernard Friedman, and James Begun. 2006. "Factors Associated with High-Quality/Low-Cost Hospital Performance." *Journal of Health Care Finance* Spring: 39-51.

Johnson, D.E. 1997. "Medical group cultures pose big challenges." *Health Care Strategic Management* 15:2-3.

Johnson, Joyce and Molly Billingsley. 1997. "Reengineering the corporate culture of hospitals." *Nursing & Health Care Perspectives* 18:316-21.

Johnson, L. 1999. "Cutting costs by managing turnover." *Balance, The Journal of the American College of Health Care Administrators.* Sept/Oct 1999 pp 21-23.

Johnson, Rep. Nancy. 2001. "Congressional Outlook: Nursing Shortages." *Hospital Outlook* 4(2): 7.

Johnson, Steven. 2001. *Emergence.* New York: Simon & Schuster.

Joiner, Keith and Steven Wormsley. 2005. "Strategies for Defining Financial Benchmarks for the Research Mission in Academic Health Centers." *Academic Medicine* 80(3): 211-217.

Joiner, Keith. 2004. "Sponsored-Research Funding by Newly Recruited Assistant Professors: Can It Be Modeled as a Sequential Series of Uncertain Events?" *Academic Medicine* 79(7): 633-643.

Joiner, Keith. 2004. "Using Utility Theory to Optimize a Salary Incentive Plan for Grant-Funded Faculty." *Academic Medicine* 79(7): 652-660.

Joiner, Keith. 2005. "A Strategy for allocating central funds to support new faculty recruitment." *Academic Medicine* 80(3): 218-224.

Jollis, James, Eric Peterson, Elizabeth DeLong, Daniel Mark, Robert Collins, Lawrence Muhlbaier, and David Pryor. 1994. "The Relation Between the Volume of Coronary Angioplasty Procedures at Hospitals Treating Medicare Beneficiaries and Short-Term Mortality." *New England Journal of Medicine* 331: 1625–29.

Jones, Walter. 2000. "The 'Business'—or 'Public Service'—of Healthcare." *Journal of Healthcare Management,* 45(5): 290-293.

Jorgensen, A. 1991. "Creating changes in the corporate culture: case study." *American Association of Occupational Health Nurses Journal* 39:319-21.

Karcz, Anita, Robert Korn, Mary Burke MC, Richard Cggiano, Michael Doyle, Michael Erdos, Errol Green, and Kenneth Williams. 1996. "Malpractice Claims Against Emergency Physicians in Massachusetts: 1975-1993." *American Journal of Emergency Medicine* 14: 341-345.

KATU.com Staff. 2013. "Man robs Portland bank for $1, wants free health care in jail." *KATU.com*

Kauffman, Stuart. 1995. *At Home in the Universe.* New York: Oxford University Press.

Kauranen, Anne. 2019. "Finland's cabinet quits over failure to deliver healthcare reform." *Reuters,* March 8.

Keeler, E.B., R.H. Brook, G.A. Goldberg, C.J. Kamberg, and J.P. Newhouse.1985 "How free care reduced hypertension in the Health Insurance Experiment." *Journal of the American Medical Association* 254: 1926-1931.

Kelly, Robert. 2014. "Public Faith in Congress Hits Historic Low." *Conventionof-states.com.*

Kennedy, Ian. 2001. "Learning from Bristol – The Report of the Public Inquiry into Children's Heart Surgery at the Bristol Royal Infirmary 1984-1995." Presented to (U.K.) Parliament by the Secretary of State for Health, July 2001.

Kessler, Daniel and Mark McClellan. 2002. "How liability law affects medical productivity." *Journal of Medical Economics* 21(6): 931-955.

KHN Staff Writer. 2012. "Study: Nearly A Third of Doctors Won't See New Medicaid Patients." *KaiserHealthNews.org.*

Kinard, Jerry and Beverly Little. 1999. "Are hospitals facing a critical shortage of skilled workers?" *Health Care Supervisor* 17(4): 54-62.

King, L. 1963. *The Growth of Medical Thought.* Chicago: University of Chicago Press.

King, et al *v.* Burwell, Secretary of Health and Human Services, et al. Supreme Court of the United States, No. 14-114 decided June 25, 2015.

Kissick, W.L. 1995. "Medicine and Management – Bridging the cultural gaps." *Physician Executive* 21:3-6.

Kite, Melissa. 2003. "Fat people will have to diet if they want to see the doctor." *London Times,* June 3.

Klein, Lloyd, Gary Schaer, James Calvin, Brian Palvas, Jill Allen, Joshua Loew, Eugene Uretz, and Joseph Parrillo. 1997. "Does Low Individual Operator Coronary Interventional Procedural Volume Correlate with Worse Institutional Procedural Outcome?" *Journal of the American College of Cardiology* 30, no. 4: 870–77.

Klienke, J.D. 1998. *Bleeding Edge-The Business of Health Care in the New Century.* Gaithersburg, MD: Aspen Publishers.

Klienke, J.D. 2005. "Dot-Gov: Market failure and the creation of a national health information technology system." *Health Affairs* 24(5): 1246-1262.

Klingle, Renee, Michael Burgoon, Walid Afifi, and Mark Callister. 1995. "Rethinking how to measure organizational culture in the hospital setting. The Hospital

Culture Scale." *Evaluation & the Health Professions* 18:166-86.

Kosmoski, K.A. and J.D. Calkin. 1986. "Critical care nurses' intent to stay in their positions." *Research in Nursing & Health* 9: 3-10.

Kotter, John and Leonard Schlesinger. 1979. "Choosing strategies for change." *Harvard Business Review* Mar-Apr 57(2): 106-114.

Kotter, John and James Heskett. 1992. *Corporate Culture and Performance*. New York: Free Press.

Kouzes, James and Barry Posner. 1997. *The Leadership Challenge*. San Francisco: Jossey-Bass.

Kraman, Steve and Ginny Hamm. 1999. "Risk management: Extreme honesty may be the best policy." *Annals of Internal Medicine* 131(12): 963-967.

Krauthammer, Charles. 1998. "Driving the best doctors away." *Washington Post*, January 9.

Krauthammer, Charles. 2015. *Things That Matter*. New York: Crown Forum.

Lacour-Gayet, Francois, David Clarke, Jeffrey Phillip Jacobs, and J. Comas. 2004. "The Aristotle Score: a complexity-adjusted method to evaluate surgical results." *European Journal of Cardio-Thoracic Surgery* 25: 911-924.

Landis, Steven. 2006. "Do the Poor deserve life support?" *Slate.com*.

Landon, Bruce, James Reschovsky, and David Blumenthal. 2003. "Changes in career satisfaction among primary care and specialist physicians, 1997-2001." *JAMA* 289(4): 442-449.

Landro, Laura. 2003. "Six prescriptions for what's ailing US Health care." *Wall Street Journal*, December 22.

Langer, Ellen. 1997. *The Power of Mindful Learning*. New York: Perseus Books.

LaPar, Damien, Castigliano Bhamidipati, Carlos Mery, George Stukenborg, David Jones, Bruce Schirmer, Irving Kron, and Gorav Ailawadi. 2010. "Primary Payer Status Affects Mortality for Major Surgical Operations." *Annals of Surgery* 252(3): 544-551.

Lazlo, Ervin. 1972. *The Systems View of the World: A Holistic Vision for Our Time (Advances in Systems Theory, Complexity, and the Human Sciences)*. New York: Braziller.

Leape, Lucian. 1994. "Error in Medicine." *JAMA* 272(3): 1851-1857.

Leonard, Devin. 2012. "Is Concierge Medicine the Future of Health Care?" *Bloomberg.com*, November 29.

Levine, Sam. 2014. "Vermont Will Stop Paying Jonathan Gruber For Health Care Work." *Huffington Post*.

Levinson, Wendy, Debra Roter, John Mullooly, Valerie Dull, and Richard Frankel. 1997. "Physician-Patient Communication: The Relationship with Malpractice Claims Among Primary Care Physicians and Surgeons." *Journal of the American Medical Association* 277: 553-559.

Levitt, Steven and Stephen Dubner. 2005. *Freakonomics—A Rogue Economist Explores the Hidden Side of Everything.* New York: Harper Collins.

Localio, A. Russell, Ann Lawthers AG, Troyen Brennan, Nan Laird, Liesi Hebert, Lynn Peterson, Joseph Newhouse, Paul Weiler, and Howard Hiatt. 1991. "Relation between malpractice claims and adverse events due to negligence: Results of the Harvard Medical Practice Study III." *New England Journal of Medicine*, 325: 245-251.

Loop, Floyd. 2001. "On medical management." *Journal of Thoracic and Cardiovascular Surgery*, 121(4): S25-S28.

Lopez-Bauman, Naomi, Rea Hederman, Lindsay Boyd Killen. 2017. "Medicaid Waiver Toolkit." State Policy Network Healthcare Working Group.

Luft, Harold, John Bunker, and Alain Enthoven. 1979. "Should operations be regionalized? The empirical relation between surgical volume and mortality." *New England Journal of Medicine*, Dec 20; 301(25): 1364-69.

Luft, Harold. 2003. "From observing the relationship between volume and outcome to making policy recommendations— Comments on Sheikh." *Medical Care* 41(10): 1118-1122.

Lurie, N., W.G. Manning, C. Peterson, G.A. Goldberg, C.A. Phelps, and L. Lilliard L. 1987. "Preventive Care: Do we practice what we preach?" *American Journal of Public Health* 77:801-804.

Luthi, Susannah. 2019. "CMS to launch new direct-contracting pay models in 2020." *ModernHealthcare.com.*

Maarse, Hans and Aggie Paulus. "Has solidarity survived? A comparative analysis of the effect of social health insurance reform in four European countries." *Journal of Health, Politics, Policy and Law* 2003; 28(4): 585-614.

Mackey, John. 2009. "The Whole Foods Alternative to Obamacare." *Wall Street Journal*, August 11.

Malcolm, Laurence, Lynn Wright, Pauline Barnett, and Chris Hendry. 2003. "Building a successful partnership between management and clinical leadership: experience from New Zealand." *British Medical Journal* 326: 653-654.

Marmot, M. 2004. The Status Syndrome—How Social Standing Affects Our Health and Longevity. Holt & Co.: New York.

Martin, Nicole. 2007. "Smokers who won't quit denied surgery." *Daily Telegraph Today* (U.K.), June 4.

Maslow, Abraham. 1943. *A theory of human motivation. Psychological Review* 50: 370-396.

Mathews, Anna. 2018. "Behind your rising health care bills: Secret hospital deals that squelch competition." *Wall Street Journal*, September 18.

McCallum, K.L. 2001. "All the good doctors always leave." *Medical Economics* 78(9): 55-6, 58, 61.

McDaniel, Reuben. 1997. "Strategic Leadership: A View from quantum and chaos theories." *Health Care Management Review* 22(1) 21-37.

McDaniel, Reuben and Dean Driebe. 2001. "Complexity Science and Health Care Management." *Advances in Health Care Management* 2: 11-36.

McFadden, Kathleen, Elizabeth Towell, and Gregory Stock. 2004. "Critical success factors for controlling and managing Hospital Errors." *Quality Management Journal* 2004; 11(1) 61-73.

McGrath, Paul, David Wennberg, David J. Malenka, Mirle A. Kellett Jr., Thomas J. Ryan Jr., John R. O'Meara, William A. Bradley, Michael J. Hearne, Bruce Hettleman, John F. Robb, Samuel Shubrooks, Peter VerLee, Matthew W. Watkins, Francis L. Lucas, Gerald T. O'Connor and for the Northern New England Cardiovascular Disease Study Group. 1998. "Operator Volume and Outcome in 12,998 Percutaneous Coronary Interventions." *Journal of American College of Cardiology* 31(3): 570–76.

McIntyre, Neil and Karl Popper. 1989. "The critical attitude in medicine: the need for a new ethics." *British Medical Journal* 287:1919- 1923.

"Medicaid at 50. 2015." Kaiser Commission on Medicaid and the Uninsured."

Meier, Barry and Katie Thomas. 2012. "Insurers Pay Big Markups When Doctors Dispense Drugs." *NYTimes.com.*

Mello, Michelle, Amitabh Chandra, Atul Gawande, and David Studdert. 2010. "National Costs of the Medical Liability System." *Health Affairs (Millwood)* Sep; 29(9): 1569-1577.

Melville, Arabella. 1980. "Job satisfaction in general practice: Implications for prescribing." *Social Sciences & Medicine* 14A (6): 495-499.

Merritt Hawkins. 2015. "Physician Access Index—A State-by-State Compilation of Benchmarks and Metrics Influencing Patient Access to Physicians and Advanced Practitioners."

Merritt Hawkins. 2017. "Survey of Physician Appointment Wait Times, 2017."

Merritt, Martin. 2013. "Why UnitedHealthcare Sent Termination Letters to Doctors in 10 States." *Physicianspractice.com*, November 24.

Messinger, Daniel, Charles R. Bauer, Abhik Das, Ron Seifer, Barry M. Lester, Linda L. Lagasse, Linda L. Wright, Seetha Shankaran, Henrietta S. Bada, Vincent L. Smeriglio, John C. Langer, Marjorie Beeghly, and W. Kenneth Poole. 2004. "The maternal lifestyle study: Cognitive, motor, and behavioral outcomes of cocaine-exposed and opiate-exposed infants through three years of age." *Pediatrics* 113: 1677-168.

Metrick, Joseph. 2000. "Organizational characteristics associated with hospital CEO turnover." *Journal of Health Care Management* 45(6): 395-404.

Meyer, Bruce D., and James X. Sullivan. 2005. "The Well-Being of Single-Mother Families After Welfare Reform." The Brookings Institution.

Millenson, Michael. 1999. *Demanding Medical Excellence: Doctors and accountability in the Information Age.* Chicago: University of Chicago Press.

Millenson, Michael. 2003. "The Silence." *Health Affairs* 22(2): 103-112.

Miller, Robert, Helene Lipton, Kathryn Saenz Duke, and Harold Luft. 1996. "Update Special Report, The San Diego Health Care System: A Snapshot of Change." *Health Affairs* 15.1: 224-229.

Miller, William, Benjamin Crabtree, Reuben McDaniel, and Kurt Stange. 1998. "Understanding change in primary care practice using complexity theory." *Journal of Family Practice* 46(5): 369-376.

Mingardi, Alberto. 2006. "A drug price path to avoid." *Washington Post,* November 10.

Mirvis, Phillip and Edward Lawler. 1977. "Measuring the financial impact of employee attitudes." *Journal of Applied Psychology* 62:1-18.

Mobley, William. 1982. *Employee Turnover: Causes, Consequences and Control.* Reading, MA: Addison-Wesley.

Moffit, Robert. 2010. "Doctors, Patients, and the New Medicare Provisions." Heritage Foundation lectures #1174 (September 23, 2010): 1-8.

Morrissey, Ed. 2012. "What free market medicine looks like." *HotAir.com,* November 15.

Mott, David. 2000. "Pharmacist job turnover, length of service, and reasons for leaving, 1983-1997." *American Journal of Health-System Pharmacy* 57(10): 975-984.

Mullaney, T.J. 2005. "This Man Wants to Heal Health Care." *Business Weekly,* October 31.

Murphy v Board of Med. Examiners, 949 P.2d 530 (Ariz. Ct. App. 1997).

Naisbitt, Doris & John. 1982. *Megatrends.* New York: Warner Books.

National Federation of Independent Business et al *v.* Sebelius, Secretary of Health and Human Services et al. Supreme Court of the United States, No. 11-393, decided June 28, 2012.

Neale, Ben. 2018. "Letter to State Medicaid Directors," dated January 11, 2018. Department of Health and Human Services.

Nelson, Dave. October 2005. Baldrige—Just What the Doctor Ordered. *Quality Progress,* pp 69-75.

NICE Manuals: "Guide to the Methods of the Technology Appraisal in the National Health Service" (U.K.)

O'Connell, Colleen. 1999. "A culture of change or a change of culture?" *Nursing Administration Quarterly* 23:65-8.

Oliver, Mike. 2015. "Judge sets trial date in $14 million Birmingham health care fraud case." *AL.com.*

Oliver, Wayne. "Kicking the Malpractice Tort Out of Court." *Wall Street Journal,* March 19.

Ollove, Michael. 2019. "States are all over the map when it comes to transgender health care." *Washington Post,* July 22.

Oostrom, Tamar, Liran Einav, and Amy Finkelstein. 2017. "Outpatient Office Wait Times and Quality of Care for Medicaid Patients." *Health Affairs* 36, no. 5 (2017): 826-832.

Orentlicher, D. 2000. "Medical Malpractice: Treating the Causes Instead of the Symptoms." *Medical Care* 38: 247-249.

Orlando Sentinel, 1998. "Doctor's Victory Revives Proponents of Quality Care." April 26.

Osnos, Evan. 2005. "In China, health care is scalpers, lines, debt." *Chicago Tribune,* September 28.

Pathman, Donald, Eric Williams, and Thomas Konrad. 1996. "Rural physician satisfaction: its sources and relation to retention." *Journal of Rural Health* 12(5): 366-377.

Pathman, Donald, Thomas Konrad, and Eric Williams. 2002. "Physician job satisfaction, dissatisfaction, and turnover." *Journal of Family Practice* 51:593.

Pearson, Steven and Michael Rawlins. 2005. "Quality, Innovation, and Value for Money: NICE and the British National Health Service." *JAMA* 294(20): 2618-2622.

Peirce, John. 2000. "The paradox of physicians and administrators in health care organizations." *Health Care Management Review* 2(1): 7-28.

Pelzman, Fred. 2014. "What being overwhelmed by rules and regulations looks like." *KevinMD.com.*

Peters, Thomas and Robert Waterman. 1982. *In Search of Excellence.* Warner Books, New York, NY.

Petrock, F. 1990. "Corporate culture enhances profits." *HR Magazine* 35:64-6.

Pfeffer, Jeffrey. 1994. *Competitive Advantage Through People.* Boston: Harvard Business School Press.

Pfeffer, Jeffrey and Robert Sutton. 2000. *The Knowing-Doing Gap.* Boston: Harvard Business School Press.

Pfeffer, Jeffrey. 2014. "Why health insurance companies are doomed." *Fortune.*

Phibbs, C.S., J.M. Bronstein, E. Buxton, and R.H. Phibbs. 1996. "The Effects of Patient Volume and Level of Care at the Hospital of Birth on Neonatal Mortality." *Journal of the American Medical Association* 276: 1054–59.

Phillips, R.I. 1974. "The informal organization in your hospital." *Radiologic Technology* 46(2): 101-106.

Pho, Kevin. 2014. "Are American doctors paid too much or too little?" *Kevinmd.com.*

Pies, Ronald. 2011. "Health Care is a Basic Human Right-- Almost Everywhere but Here." *OpEdNews.*

Pollitz, Karen. 2017. "High-Risk Pools for Uninsurable Individuals." Kaiser Family Foundation.

Porter, L.W., R.M. Steers, R.T. Mowday, and P.V. Boulian. 1974. "Organizational commitment, job satisfaction, and turnover among psychiatric technicians." *Journal of Applied Psychology* 59(5): 603-609.

Porter, Michael and Elizabeth Olmsted Teisberg. 2006. *Redefining Health Care— Creating Value-Based Competition on Results.* Boston: Harvard Business School Publishing.

Prescott, Patricia. 1986. "Vacancy, stability, and turnover of registered nurses in hospitals." *Research in Nursing & Health* 9: 51-60.

Price, James and Charles Mueller. 1981. "A causal model of turnover for nurses." *Academy of Management Journal* 24(3): 543-565.

Proenca, E. Jose. 1996. "Market orientation and organizational culture in hospitals." *Journal of Hospital Marketing* 11:3-18.

Provan, K.G. July 1984. "Interorganizational cooperation and decision making autonomy in a consortium multi-hospital system." *Academy of Management Review* 9(3): 494-504.

Public Law 89-97. 1965. "Hospital Insurance Program." (original Medicaid law).

Public Law 104–193. 1996. "Personal Responsibility and Work Opportunity Reconciliation Act" enacted by 104th Congress of the United States.

Public Law 111-148. 2010. "Patient Protection and Affordable Care Act" enacted by 111th Congress of the United States.

Public testimony before Texas legislature on July 25, 2017. Texas Government Code. 2011. Medicaid Reform Waiver, Title 4, Subtitle I, Chapter 537.

Quigley, William. 2001. "London Report: Medical missteps compound in child's death." *Albuquerque Journal*, December 17.

Quigley, William. 2002. "The health of health care." (Quoting Martin Hickey, former Lovelace CEO.) *Albuquerque Journal*, October 28.

Rael, Hannah. 2016. "State to Provide Healthcare Services to All Children Regardless of Immigration Status." *Noozhawk.com*.

Rand Health. 2005. "Future Health and Medical Care Spending of the Elderly – Implications for Medicare."

Rasmussen, Tom. 2005. "A Mandated Burden." *Wall Street Journal*, July 29.

Reinhardt, Uwe. 2011. "Would privatizing Medicare lead to better cost controls?" *New York Times*, May 18.

Report to Congress: Improving Incentives in the Medicare Program, June 2009. Medicare Payment Advisory Commission, Washington, DC.

Reuters. 2014. "Cigarette smoking costs weigh heavily on the healthcare system."

Roberts, Genevieve. 2005. "Overweight patients to be denied NHS hip operations." *London Times*, November 23.

Rogers, Everett. 1983. *Diffusion of Innovation*. New York: The Free Press.

Rosenberg, Tina. "Revealing a Health Care Secret: The Price." *NYTimes.com*, July 31.

Rosenthal, Elizabeth. 2017. *An American Sickness—How healthcare became big business and how you can take it back*. Penguin Books: New York.

Rowe, Kyle, Whitney Rowe, Josh Umbehr, Frank Dong, and Elizabeth Ablah. 2017. "Direct Primary Care in 2015: A Survey with Selected Comparisons to 2005 Survey Data." *Kansas Journal of Medicine* 10(1): 3-6.

Roy, Avik. 2010. "UVa Study: Surgical Patients on Medicaid Are 13% More Likely to Die Than Those Without Insurance." *National Review*.

Rubin, Rita. May 2, 2018. "Is Direct Primary Care a Game Changer?" *J Amer Med Assoc*.

Rucci, Anthony, Steven Kirn, and Richard Quinn. 1998. "The employee-customer-profit chain at Sears." *Harvard Business Review* Jan/Feb, 83-97.

Sackett, D.L., W.M. Rosenberg, J.A. Gray, R.B. Haynes, and W.S. Richardson. 1996. "Evidence based medicine: what it is and what it isn't." *British Medical Journal* 312(7023): 71-2.

Scherz, Hal. 2013. "Healthcare Reform for Thee, But Not Me." *Townhall.com*, September 25.

Schwartz, William and Neil Komesar. 1978. "Doctors, Damages and Deterrence." *New England Journal of Medicine* 298: 1282- 1289.

Scott, Tim, Russell Mannion, Huw Davies, and Martin Marshall. 2003. "The Quantitative Measurement of Organizational Culture in Health Care: A Review of the Available Instruments." *Health Services Research* 38(3): 923-38.

Seago, J. 1997. "Organizational Culture in Hospitals: Issues in Measurement." *Journal of Nursing Measurement* 5 (2): 165-78.

Senge, Peter. 1990. *The Fifth Discipline-The Art and Practice of the Learning Organization.* New York: Currency Doubleday.

Sfikas, Peter. 1998. "Are Insurers Making Treatment Decisions?" *JADA* 129: 1036-1039.

Shanahan, Mary. 1993. "A comparative analysis of recruitment and retention of health care professionals." *Health Care Management Review* 18(3): 41-51.

Sheikh, A. and B. Hurwitz. 1999. "A national database of medical errors." *Journal of the Royal Society of Medicine* November 92: 554-555.

Sheikh, K. 2003. Reliability of provider volume and outcome associations for healthcare policy. *Medical Care* October, 41(10): 1111-1117.

Shortell, Stephen. Fall 1988. The evolution of hospital systems: Unfulfilled promises and self-fulfilling prophecies. *Medical Care Review* 45: 745-772.

Shortell, Stephen, Robin Gillies, David Anderson, James Mitchell, and Kerry Morgan. 1993. "Creating organized delivery systems: The barriers and facilitators." *Hospital & Health Services Administration* 38(4): 447-466.

Shortell, Stephen. 1997. Commentary on: "Physician-Hospital integration and the economic theory of the firm" by JC Robinson. *Medical Care Research and Review* 54:3-24.

Shortell, Stephen, Charles Bennett, and Gayle Byck. 1998. "Assessing the impact of continuous quality improvement on clinical practice: What it will take to accelerate progress." *Millbank Quarterly* 76(4): 593-624.

Shortell, Stephen, Teresa Waters, Kenneth Clarke, and Peter Budetti. 1998. "Physicians as double agents: Maintaining trust in an era of multiple accountabilities." *JAMA* 23: 1102-1108.

Shortell, Stephen, Robin Gillies, David Anderson, Karen Morgan Erickson, and John Mitchell. 2000. *Remaking Health Care in America: The Evolution of Organized Delivery Systems.* San Francisco: Jossey-Bass.

Shortell, Stephen, Robert Jones, A.W. Rademaker, and Robin Gillies. 2000. "Assessing the Impact of Total Quality management and Organizational Culture on Multiple Outcomes of Care for Coronary Artery Bypass Graft Surgery Patients." *Medical Care* 38 (2): 207-17.

Simone, Joseph. 1999. "Understanding Academic Medical Centers: Simone's Maxims." *Clinical Cancer Research* 5:2281-2285.

Smith, Gordon and Jill Pell. 2003. "Parachute use to prevent death and major trauma related to gravitational challenge: systematic review of randomized controlled trials." *British Medical Journal* 327: 1459-61.

Smith, George. 2008. "Accessing health care resources: Economic, Medical, Ethical and Socio-legal challenges." In: Weisstub D.N. and G. Diaz Pintos. *Autonomy and Human Rights in Health Care.* The Netherlands: Springer.

Smith, Howard Lee, Steven Yourstone, David Lorber, and Bruce Mann. 2001. "Managed care and medical practice guidelines: The thorny problem of attaining physician compliance." In: *Advances in Health Care Management,* Vol II, New York: Elsevier Science.

Smith, Howard Lee, Deane Waldman, Marvin Fottler, Jacqueline Hood. 2005. "Chapter 5: Strategic Management of Internal Customers: Building Value through Human Capital and Culture." In: *Advances in Health Care Management, Volume 6: Strategic Thinking and Entrepreneurial Action in the Health Care Industry.* Bingley, West Yorkshire, England: Emerald Insight.

Soffel, D. and Harold Luft. 1993. "Anatomy of health care reform proposals." *Western Journal of Medicine* 159: 494-500.

Spear, Steven. 2005. "Fixing Healthcare from the Inside, Today." *Harvard Business Review,* September pp. 2-16.

Staff. 2019. "New bill looks to clear path for state universal health care." *MyNorthwest.com,* February 14.

Steiger, Bill. 2006. "Survey Results: Doctors Say Morale Is Hurting." *Physician Executive.* Nov/Dec pp. 6-15.

Sterman, John. 2002. "Systems dynamics modeling: Tools for learning in a complex world." *IEEE Engineering Management Review* First Quarter pp. 42-52.

Sterman, John. 2006. "Learning from evidence on a complex world." *American Journal of Public Health* 96: 505-514.

Stevenson, K. 2000. "Are your Practices Resistant to Changing Their Clinical Culture?" *Primary Care Report* 2 (5): 19-20.

Stocking, Barbara. 1992. "Promoting change in clinical care." *Quality in health care* 1: 56-60.

Stoller, James, Douglas Orens, and Lucy Kester. 2001. "The impact of turnover among respiratory care practitioners in a health care system: Frequency and associated costs." *Respiratory Care* 46(3): 238-242.

Stossel, T. and D. Shaywitz. July 9, 2006. "Biotech Bucks Don't Corrupt Researchers." Reprinted from the *Washington Post* in the *Albuquerque Journal*, Page B3.

Stout, Mary Katherine. 2006. "Medicaid: Yesterday, Today and Tomorrow—A short history of Medicaid Policy and its impact on Texas." Texas Public Policy Foundation.

Strawn, Julie, Mark Greenberg, and Steve Savner. 2001. *Improving Employment Outcomes Under TANF*. Center for Law and Social Policy.

Stubblefield, Al. 2005. *The Baptist Healthcare Journey to Excellence*. Hoboken, N.J.: Wiley & Sons.

Studdert, David, Eric Thomas, Helen Burstin, Brett Zbar, E. Orav, and Troyen Brennan. 2000. "Negligent Care and Malpractice Claiming Behavior in Utah and Colorado." *Medical Care* 38: 250-260.

Suderman, Peter. 2017. "More Than 10 Percent of Federal Medicaid Payments Last Year Were Improper." *Reason.com*.

Surowiecki, James. 2004. *The Wisdom of Crowds*. New York: Anchor Books.

Tai, Teresa, Sherry Bame, and Chester Robinson. 1998. "Review of nursing turnover research, 1977-1996." *Society of Science in Medicine*. 47(12): 1905-1924.

Taragin, Mark, Frank Sonnenberg, M. Elizabeth Karns, Richard Trout, Sharona Shapiro, and Jeffrey Carson. 1994. "Does Physician Performance Explain Interspecialty Differences in Malpractice Claim Rates?" *Medical Care* 32: 661-667.

Tate, Nick. 2012. *Obamacare Survival Guide*. West Palm Beach, FL: Humanix Books.

Texas, et al v. United States of America, et al, Civil Action No. 4:18-cv-00167-0, United States District Court for the Northern District of Texas Fort Worth Division, December 14, 2018.

TMA (Texas Medical Association). 2017. "TMA Survey Results, 2017 and Previous Years."

Tribus, Marvin. 1992. The germ theory of management. *National Institute for Engineering Management & Systems*, Publication #1459

Tribus, Marvin. February 1992. Reducing Deming's 14 Points to practice. *Quality First*. National Institute for Engineering Management and Systems, NSPE Publication #1459

Trigg, Barbara. 2011. "Make Health Care A Right for All." *Albuquerque Journal*, February 25.

Tullis, Paul. May 10, 2017. "Can California Go Single-Payer?" *The American Prospect*.

Turner, Grace-Marie. 2014. "The Human Tragedy of Obamacare's Job Losses." *Forbes*, February 6.

Ungar, Rick. 2012. "Obesity Now Costs Americans More in HealthCare Spending Than Smoking." *Forbes*, April 30.

"U.S. national health expenditure as percent of GDP from 1960 to 2019." *Statista.com*.

Uttal, Bro. 1983. "The Corporate Culture Vultures." *Fortune* October 17, pp. 66-72.

Uyttebrouck, Oliver. 2014. "Nursing shortage forces VA hospital in ABQ to cut beds." *Albuquerque Journal*, October 21.

Van der Merwe, R. and S. Miller. 1971. The Measurement of Labour Turnover." *Human Relations* 24(3): 233-253.

Veghte, Ben. 2014. "Health Care Consumes Over a Third of Social Security Checks." *HuffingtonPost.com*.

Verma, Seema. "Letter: Seema Verma to Jon Hamdorf." May 7, 2018.

Veterans Health Administration. 2015. "Review of Alleged Mismanagement at the Health Eligibility Center." VA Office of Inspector General, 14-01792-510.

Vitkine, Benoit. 2012. "Inside the dramatic collapse of Greece's healthcare system." *BusinessInsider.com*.

Volk, JoAnn and Justin Giovannelli. 2017. "Who Would Gain Under the Proposal to Expand Health Savings Accounts?" *Commonwealthfund.com*.

Von Drehle, David. 2014. "Medicine Is About to Get Personal." *Time.com*.

Vought, Mary. 2019. "My daughter's medication isn't available for patients in Britain's single-payer system." *USAToday.com*, June 15.

Waldman, Deane, Terri Young, Stanley Pappelbaum, Searle Turner, Stanley Kirkpatrick, and Lily George. 1982. "Pediatric cardiac catheterization with 'same-day' discharge." *American Journal of Cardiology* 50:800- 804.

Waldman, Deane, Stanley Pappelbaum, and Lily George. 1984. "Cost-containment strategies in congenital heart disease." *Western Journal of Medicine* 141:123-126.

Waldman, Deane, Richard Ratzan, and Stanley Pappelbaum. 1998. "Physicians must abandon the *illusion* of autonomy...." *Pediatric Cardiology* 19:9-17.

Waldman, Deane and Richard Spector. 2003. "Malpractice claims analysis yields widely applicable principles." *Pediatric Cardiology* 24(2): 109-117.

Waldman, Deane, Howard Lee Smith, and Jacqueline Hood. 2003. "Corporate Culture — The missing piece of the healthcare puzzle." *Hospital Topics* 81(1): 5-14.

Waldman, Deane and Franklin Schargel. 2003. "Twins in Trouble: The need for system-wide reform of both Healthcare and Education." *Total Quality Management & Business Excellence,* October 14(8): 895-901.

Waldman, Deane, Steven Yourstone, and Howard Lee Smith. 2003. "Learning Curves in Healthcare." *Health Care Management Review* 28(1): 43-56.

Waldman, Deane, Howard Lee Smith, Frank Kelly, and Sanjeev Arora. 2004. "The Shocking Cost of Turnover in Healthcare." *Health Care Management Review* 29(1): 2-7.

Waldman, Deane and Sanjeev Arora. 2004. "Retention rather than turnover—A Better and Complementary HR Method." *Human Resource Planning* 27(3): 6-9.

Waldman, Deane and Franklin Schargel. 2006. "Twins in Trouble (II): Systems Thinking in Healthcare and Education." *Total Quality Management & Business Excellence* 17(1): 117-130.

Waldman, Deane, Sanjeev Arora, Howard Lee Smith, and Jacqueline Hood. 2006. "Improving medical practice outcomes by retaining clinicians." *Journal of Medical Practice Management* March/April pp. 263-271.

Waldman, Deane. 2006. "Change the Metrics: If *you get what you measure,* then measure what you want—retention." *Journal of Medical Practice Management* July/August, pp. 1-7.

Waldman, Deane, Jacqueline Hood, and Howard Lee Smith. 2006. "Healthcare CEO and Physician—Reaching Common Ground." *Journal of Healthcare Management.* May/June 51(3): 171-187.

Waldman, Deane, Steven Yourstone, and Howard Lee Smith. 2007. "Learning-The Means to Improve Medical Outcomes." *Health Services Management Research* 20: 227-237.

Waldman, Deane and Kenneth Cohn. 2007. "Mend the Gap." In: *The Business of Health,* Editors: KH Cohn & D Hough, New York: Praeger Perspectives.

Waldman, Deane. 2009. "The Triple Standard in Healthcare." *California Journal of Politics & Policy* 1(1): 1-13.

Waldman, Deane. 2010. *Uproot U.S. Healthcare.* Albuquerque, NM: ADM Books.

Waldman, Deane. 2010. *Cambio Radical al Sistema de Salud de los Estados Unidos.* Albuquerque, NM: ADM Books.

Waldman, Deane. 2013. "The Health of Healthcare (I) — The Right Approach is Medical." *J Med Pract Med,* July/August, pp. 29-31.

Waldman, Deane. 2013. *The Cancer in Healthcare – How Greed Is Killing What We Love*. Denver: Hugo House Publishers.

Waldman, Deane. 2013. " The Health of Healthcare (II)– Healthcare Has Cancer." *Journal of Medical Practice Management* Sept/Oct Pages 113-116.

Waldman, Deane. 2013. "The Health of Healthcare (III) – Dissolving (Curing) the Cancer in Healthcare." *Journal of Medical Practice Management* Nov/Dec, Pages 184-186.

Waldman, Deane. 2014. "The U.S. Needs Tort Replacement, Not Just 'Reform.'" *Journal of Socialomics* 3:107.

Waldman, Deane. 2014. "The Health of Healthcare (V) – Is the Very Freedom of Providers At Risk?" *J Med Pract Med*, May/June, Vol. 29, No. 6, Pp. 366-368.

Waldman, Deane. 2014. "The Health of Healthcare (VI) – Be Prepared!" *Journal of Medical Practice Management* July/August, Pp. 64-66.

Waldman, Deane. 2015. "Bureaucracy, not drugs, drives health costs." *Wall Street Journal*, December 21.

Waldman, Deane. 2015. *Our Allies Have Become our Enemies*, ebook #1 in, *Restoring Care to American Healthcare*. Columbus, OH: Gatekeeper Press.

Waldman, Deane. 2016. *Washington's BARRC Is Its Bite*, ebook #2 in, *Restoring Care to American Healthcare*. Columbus, OH: Gatekeeper Press.

Waldman, Deane. 2016. *The Root Cause That Washington Conceals*, ebook #3 in, *Restoring Care to American Healthcare*. Columbus, OH: Gatekeeper Press.

Waldman, Deane. 2016. *Is Obamacare the Answer?*, ebook #4 in e-series, *Restoring Care to American Healthcare*. Columbus, OH: Gatekeeper Press.

Waldman, Deane. 2016. *Single Payer Won't Save Us*, ebook #5 in e-series, *Restoring Care to American Healthcare*. Columbus, OH: Gatekeeper Press.

Waldman, Deane. 2016. "Government Hypocrisy over Epipen: The Pot Calling the Kettle Black." *Forbes*.

Waldman, Deane. 2016. "The Great Disruptor Can Fix Healthcare." *The Hill*.

Waldman, Deane. 2016. "Obamacare's Dangerous Wait Lines." *The Hill*.

Waldman, Deane. 2017. "Healthcare Regulations are Hazardous to your Health." *The Hill*.

Waldman, Deane. 2017. "Texas and Medicaid: How big can you dream?" *Tribune Talk.org*.

Waldman, Deane. 2017. "The Saga of 1115—A Waiver Can Fix Texas Medicaid, But Only Temporarily." Texas Public Policy Foundation.

Waldman, Deane. 2017. "Who knows Texans best: Washington or Texas?" *Midland Reporter-Telegram.*

Waldman, Deane. 2017. "Administrative job growth in healthcare isn't good for America." *The Hill.*

Waldman, Deane. 2017. "More coverage doesn't necessarily translate into better patient care." *The Hill.*

Waldman, Deane and Vance Ginn. 2017. "California and Texas Agree on Health Care." *Real Clear Health.*

Waldman, Deane. 2017. "Think Obamacare Is Bad? 'Medicare for All' Would Make Things Even Worse." *Daily Signal.*

Waldman, Deane. 2018. "Americans can be entitled or free—but not both." *The Hill.*

Waldman, Deane. 2018. "Texas deserves credit for running health care the right way." *The Hill.*

Waldman, Deane. 2018. "Great Britain Offers Cautionary Tale on Single Payer." *Real Clear Health.*

Waldman, Deane. 2018. "Conflating Health Insurance with Health Care." *Real Clear Health.*

Waldman, Deane. 2018. "Medicare for All is a socialist's dream — and an American Nightmare." *The Hill.*

Waldman, Deane and Jennifer Minjarez. 2019. "Extend Gains from Welfare Reform to Texas Medicaid." Texas Public Policy Foundation.

Waldman, Deane and Jennifer Minjarez. 2019. "Extend Gains from Welfare Reform to Texas Medicaid." Texas Public Policy Foundation.

Waldman, Deane. 2019. "Effect on patient care of H.R. 1384, 'Medicare-for-All.'" Texas Public Policy Foundation.

Waldman, Deane. Forthcoming. *We Need Tort Replacement, Not Reform*, ebook #7 in, *Restoring Care to American Healthcare.* Columbus, OH: Gatekeeper Press.

Walker, Jan, Eric Pan, Douglas Johnston, Julia Adler-Milstein, David Bates, and Blackford Middleton. 2005. "The Value of Health Care Information Exchange and Interoperability." *Health Affairs.* W 5—10-18.

Walshe, Kieran and Thomas Rundall. 2001. "Evidence-based management: From theory to practice in health care." *Millbank Quarterly,* 79(3): 429.

Ward, Bryce, and Brandon Bridge. 2018. *The Economic Impact of Medicaid Expansion in Montana.* University of Montana Bureau of Business and Economic Research.

Watts, Alan. 1951. *The Wisdom of Insecurity.* New York: Pantheon Books.

Weil, T.P. 1987. "The changing relationship between physicians and the hospital CEO." *Trustee*, Feb; 40(2): 15-18.

Weil, Peter. 1990. "Job turnover of CEOs in teaching and nonteaching hospitals." *Academic Med*, 65(1): 1-7.

Weisman, Carol, Cheryl Alexander, and Gary Chase. 1981. "Determinants of hospital staff nurse turnover." *Medical Care* 19(4): 431-443.

Wilson, L. 2004. "Healthier habits will reduce medical costs." *Albuquerque Journal*, July 22.

Wittkower, E.D. and W.J. Stauble. 1972. "Psychiatry and the general practitioner." *Psychiatry Med* 3:287-301.

Woods, Thomas. 2009. *Meltdown*. Washington, D.C.: Regenery Publishing.

Wu, Albert, T.A. Cavanaugh. S.J. McPhee, and Bernard Lo, and G.P. Micco. 1997. "To tell the truth—Ethical and Practical Issues in disclosing medical mistakes to patients." *Journal of General Internal Medicine* 12: 770-775.

Wysocki, Bernard. 2004. "To fix health care, hospitals take tips from factory floor." *Wall Street Journal*, April 9.

Young, Gary, Martin Charns, Jennifer Daley, Maureen Forbes, William Henderson, and Shukri Khuri.. "Best Practices for Managing Surgical Services: The Role of Coordination." *Health Care Management Review* 1997; 22(4): 72-81.

Younossi, Zobair. 2018. "HCV outcomes worse for patients with public insurance, Medicaid." *Digestive Disease Weekly*, June 3.

Zoppo, Avalon, Amanda Santos, and Jackson Hudgins. 2017. "Here's the Full List of Donald Trump's Executive Orders," *NBC News*.

Zuger, Abigail. 2004. "Dissatisfaction with Medical Practice." *New England Journal of Medicine* 350(1): 69-76.

Dr. Deane's Healthcare Decoder

Dr. Deane Waldman's Healthcare Decoder is purely functional. It takes the mystery and confusion out of healthcare and replaces them with understanding. Whether the complexity is intentional or not, the language and terms people use in healthcare are often confusing and make no sense. Sometimes they mean the opposite of what you think they mean. This Decoder does precisely what you want it to do: it decodes. It turns healthcare gibberish into easy-to-understand language.

Healthcare versus **health care** = As one word, *healthcare* means a huge system that consumes nearly 20 percent of the U.S. annual GDP. *Health care*—two words—refers to a close personal (fiduciary) service relationship, protected by law, between a patient and a provider.

ACA = Affordable Care Act, also known colloquially as Obamacare. Keep in mind the law's full name—Patient Protection and Affordable Health Care Act of 2010 (PPAHCA)—to remember what it was supposed to do for us.

Adverse impact = when a patient is harmed during, not necessarily by, health care. This is a negative patient outcome, such as failure to improve, or being sicker or worse after treatment. Contrast this *outcome* or result to the words "error" or "mistake," which refer to a *behavior* or action, not an outcome. You can read details about the important difference between behavior and outcome in *The Cancer in the American Healthcare System*. (*See* error/mistake.)

Adverse selection = when an insurance carrier has a large number of sick enrollees, who therefore require the carrier to pay large medical bills. This is "adverse," i.e., a negative result, for the insurance company's bottom line. With enough adverse selection, an insurance carrier could lose enough money paying medical claims to go bankrupt. Before this happens, a carrier will simply stop selling medical insurance, as several have already done.

APTC = **A**dvanced Premium **T**ax **C**redit, more commonly known as "ACA subsidies." This refers to the money offered by the federal government to offset increased cost of health insurance premiums. There is a sliding scale for the amount of subsidy from 400 percent of the poverty line ($93,132 per year) to 138 percent of the poverty line ($23,283). Between 138 percent and 400 percent, you get a subsidy, but less as your income increases. Above 400 percent, there is no subsidy. Below 138 percent of the poverty line, you are eligible for free insurance through Medicaid, assuming you are a legal citizen. Under the ACA, 79 percent of the U.S. population qualifies for some amount of subsidy. Median household income in the United States in September 2014 was $51,939.

Balance billing = a practice where the provider bills the patient for the difference between what insurance pays and the actual charges.

BARRC = **B**ureaucracy, **A**dministration, **R**ules, **R**egulations, and **C**ompliance. Acronym that stands for what a bureaucracy is and does.

Benefit = services or items that the insurance coverage will pay for. It does not guarantee that you will actually receive the benefit, only that *if you can get* the covered care, the insurer will pay a contracted amount to the provider.

BigPharma=a common nickname for huge, usually multinational pharmaceutical companies, such as GlaxoSmithKline, Johnson & Johnson, Merck, Pfizer, and Roche.

Bureaucracy = excessively complicated administrative process or system. For my purposes, "bureaucracy" includes (1) administration such as eligibility confirmation, billing, coding, payment, and distribution; (2) insurance activities from actuarial analysis to authorization; and (3) the regulatory machine from rule making through the review process to compliance oversight and accreditation or loss of accreditation.

Burwell v. Hobby Lobby: See SCOTUS.

Butterfly effect = is a crude way of describing the Law of Disproportionate Consequences. This "law" states that small actions can have big outcomes, and conversely, grand actions can have trivial or insignificant results. As an example in healthcare, consider the massive effort and huge expense of Obamacare, which produced little or no beneficial effect for We the Patients.

Cadillac tax = part of PPAHCA. It levies a 40 percent tax on any insurance premium that costs annually more than $10,200 for an individual or $27,500 for a family. This tax has little to do with personal income and everything to do with benefits of the insurance plan. The Cadillac tax will hit those in high-risk occupations such as construction workers, firefighters, and police officers.

Cancer = where a previously healthy cell in a human body or part of a system no longer performs its normal functions and begins to grow uncontrollably, ultimately killing the person or the system.

CBO (contrast to GAO) = the **C**ongressional **B**udget **O**ffice, tasked with predicting the *future* economic and budgetary effects of congressional action. It is primarily responsible to the executive branch of government.

In a sense, the CBO is a fiscal watchdog for actions taken by the legislative branch. For example, the CBO has calculated the future cost of PPAHCA as low as $1.1 trillion and as high as $1.7 trillion. (*See* GAO.)

CCIIO (pronounced sis-eye-oh) = the Center for Consumer Information and Insurance Oversight. CCIIO is another federal agency that creates and oversees insurance rules and compliance with healthcare regulations, specifically with the Affordable Care Act (ACA).

Charge = the price, or what you see on a bill for payment. This has no relationship, repeat *no relationship*, to what is actually paid or the true cost.

CLASS Act = The Community Living Assistance Services and Support Act was Title VII in the ACA. It was intended to create a voluntary, public, long-term-care insurance program, but was deleted from the act by the White House seven months after the ACA was signed into law.

CMS = Centers for Medicare & Medicaid Services. This is the federal agency that funds and oversees both programs.

COBRA = Consolidated Omnibus Budget Reconciliation Act of 1985. Allows a patient to keep insurance temporarily after employment ends. The employer no longer pays any portion of the premium: the insured pays 100 percent plus an administrative fee. There are other restrictions.

Complexity = the state of being complex, which, according to the dictionary, means "composed of many different and connected parts." It also means "not easy to understand." Complexity in healthcare comes in two forms: inherent and artificial.

Compliance over science = following the rules is more important than the patient. If a clinical guideline says one thing but the latest data or a doctor's well-honed judgment says something different, the doctor must follow the approved clinical pathway.

Concierge medicine = a form of "direct-pay medicine." "Concierge" doctors contract with patients for direct payments but also accept insurance. Cash-only physicians, also a form of direct-pay, do not accept insurance at all. This usually involves a retainer fee that covers office visits. Most direct-pay practices negotiate large discounts at labs and with hospitals as well as pharmacies, because the patients will pay cash. By cutting out the insurance carriers, these practices dramatically reduce both their administrative expenses and the time doctors spend on bureaucratic nonsense.

Consumer = In both health care, the service, and healthcare, the system, the consumer is the patient. Personally, I dislike the word "consumer," as it refers to a purely one-way relationship: doctor delivers and patient consumes. We all know that good medicine is a two-way relationship, a partnership, not a delivery service.

It is important to recognize that healthcare is currently a third-party payer system, meaning that the *consumer* of goods and services is not the *payer* for the goods and services consumed. She or he does not pay the supplier (provider) of services and goods—the third party does. Thus, there is micro-economic disconnection, where supply and demand—normally connected by supplier competition and demander's (consumer's) money—are *disconnected*. This prevents the functioning of free-market forces. (*See* micro-economic disconnection.)

CO-OP = Consumer Operated & Oriented Plan established by the ACA law. Co-ops are not-for-profit insurance companies that were given large sums of taxpayer dollars—more than $2.4 billion in low-interest loans (down from the initial $6 billion)—by the federal government to offer low-cost alternatives to insurance products sold by commercial for- profit companies. These co-ops are not co-ops in the usual sense, as the customers do not participate in profits and losses. As of June 2016, 13 of the 23 ACA-established insurance co-ops have either closed or been declared insolvent. Nine of the remaining 10 are near insolvency. ACA co-ops are going out of business because of simple economics: they are paying out more in mandated benefits than they are taking in as revenue.

Co-pay (insurance term) = a payment you make to the doctor, typically $5–20, when you go for care. This is in addition to what the insurance company will pay the doctor on your behalf for your care services and in addition to the cost of your premiums.

Cosmology episode = a condition when the world makes no sense—when, for instance, the sun rises out of the south. This is what providers of health care face every day. They think they are doing what patients want and yet the "system" in which they work obstructs, constrains, and punishes them. This makes no sense—care providers experience the healthcare system as a cosmology episode every minute of every day.

Cost = is the most misunderstood and, therefore, misused word in healthcare language. You and I use "cost" to mean the sum of all materials, labor, and capital to produce a product or service. Using that definition, no one knows the cost of anything in health care as well as healthcare. In the world of healthcare, "cost" is allocated, apportioned, back-calculated, and projected, but not the simple sum of all factors of production and distribution. Be sure you understand that anyone who claims to report the true cost of anything in healthcare is guessing.

Cost-sharing reduction (CSR) = there are two forms of CSR and they are quite different. There are *patient* CSRs, where the patient must pay a portion of the bill for service in addition to what was paid as a premium. There are *federal* CSRs, where Congress will subsidize the expenses of an insurance company, trying to reduce the premium costs that patients will pay. Federal CSRs are also known as "bailouts."

Covered life = someone who has signed up with a qualified health plan for insurance. As soon as the insurance card is issued, the person is covered for 90 days, even if that individual does not pay the premiums.

Debt versus deficit (U.S. national) = often confused with each other, but quite different. The *deficit* is the amount the government spends per year beyond the amount the government takes in as revenue. For the past 10 years, the deficit has been approximately 30 percent, meaning that if we took in $2 trillion, we spent $3 trillion. To cover the annual deficit, each year the government must borrow the amount of the deficit. This accumulated borrowing is called the national *debt*, which has increased from $7 trillion (2004) to $12 trillion (2009) to $19 trillion (2016). The 2018 national debt is approaching $21 trillion. Eventually, someone will have to pay this back. Meanwhile, the public pays debt service on the national debt. In 2015, just the service on this debt cost us $400 billion.

Deductible (insurance term) = a predetermined amount of money you must pay before your insurance company will pay your claim. This is in addition to the cost of your premiums.

Defensive medicine = when providers make decisions based on how their record will look, not necessarily on what is best for the patient.

Diagnosis = literally means "the identification of the *nature* of an illness." Nature can mean only the description of the ailment, and/or it can mean the root cause of your problem. Many, in fact most, diagnoses are descriptive, not etiologic. (*See* root cause.)

Dissolve (a problem) = is the most desirable of the four ways to "solve" a problem. It is described in detail in *The Cancer in the American Healthcare System*. To dissolve a problem means you change the system so the root cause of the problem no longer exists. Therefore, the problem cannot recur because the root cause is gone.

"Donut hole" = a gap in coverage in Medicare (Part D) where the beneficiary has to pay all of his or her prescription drug costs. The gap is between where the initial, minimum coverage ends and when the beneficiary has spent enough to reach the catastrophic coverage threshold.

Down-code = use of a billing code by a health care provider to give a reduced rate for health care services or goods provided. Believe it or not, this is illegal.

Effectiveness (contrast to efficiency) = refers to how successful a person, organization, or system is in achieving the desired effect. In baseball, an effective pitcher is one who throws strikes that people cannot hit. An effective healthcare system makes and keeps the most people as healthy and as long-lived as possible. *An effective system is always efficient, but an efficient one may not be effective.*

Efficiency (contrast to effectiveness) = is classically defined in terms of work per unit time, but it really means using the least resources (money, labor, power) while working. You can be very efficient and still be ineffective. If you can produce 10 buggy whips per hour but nobody wants to buy them, you are highly efficient but not effective (at producing income for your company). In healthcare, if you see 10 patients per hour, you are very efficient. If they all remain ill, you are NOT effective.

EHB = Essential Health Benefits. This is a federally mandated list of health services that an insurance plan must offer in order to be compliant with the ACA.

Employer mandate = a law that requires businesses with 50 or more full-time employees to provide health insurance to at least 95 percent of their employees and dependents up to age 26. If they don't, employers have to pay some steep fees, which can be as high as $2,000 per month per uninsured employee.

EMR = Electronic Medical Record. This system converts hard-copy records and prescriptions to digital format. As users, doctors and nurses find EMR quite *unfriendly*; it is overly cumbersome, excessively time-consuming, and extreme costly. Time required to utilize EMR is time the provider cannot spend with the patient or researching the case.

EMTALA = Emergency Medical Treatment and Labor Act of 1986, also known as the "anti-dumping law." This requires emergency rooms to care for (rather than transfer) any acutely, seriously ill patient, regardless of whether the patient has any payment source or not. EMTALA created the *unfunded mandate*.

Enrollment period (for buying insurance) = a limited amount of time, usually two to three months, when you are allowed to buy or make changes to your health insurance. The rest of the year you cannot purchase government-supported health insurance.

Entitlement = a legal right or just claim to receive or do something. Most people use the words "right" and "entitlement" interchangeably, assuming both are free (no payment) and that everyone gets their right or entitlement whenever they want regardless of income, location, age, and, for health care, regardless of whether they are citizens or not.

ERISA = Employee Retirement Income Security Act of 1974. Creates standards for employer-sponsored health insurance plans, especially those that are self-funded. Many large organizations, from large hospitals to Walmart and Amazon, are self-funded for health insurance. ERISA rules supersede any state-level insurance rules.

Error/mistake (contrast to adverse impact) = an incorrect action or behavior. To make an error requires that the correct action or behavior is known and possible. So, in healthcare, if there is no medical choice that is proven to be "correct," then there cannot be a mistake, even if a patient has an adverse impact. (*See* adverse impact.)

Exemption (or waiver) = release of an organization, group, or even municipality from having to comply with the legal requirements of PPAHCA. Certain religious groups and more than 1,400 organizations—unions or businesses—have been granted exemptions.

FFM = **F**ederally **F**acilitated **M**arketplace. This is the federally run program, created by PPAHCA, in which American citizens can and must purchase health insurance. The website's URL is www.healthcare.gov.

FPL = **F**ederal **P**overty **L**evel. This is a measure of income determined each year by the Department of Health and Human Services. The FPL is used as a baseline to define eligibility for Medicaid and CHIP, amongst other federal social programs. In 2017, the FPL for a family of four was $28,290. With ACA setting Medicaid eligibility up to 138 percent of FPL, a family qualified with income less than $39,040.

Fiduciary = a relationship between two people in which person A gives control over himself or herself to person B so that B can use this power for the benefit of person A.

GAO= **G**overnment **A**ccounting **O**ffice. Whereas the Congressional Budget Office (CBO) is concerned with the future, the GAO, also called the "Congressional watchdog," looks at the past. This agency assesses federal spending. For instance, in 1990 on the twenty-fifth anniversary of the Medicare Act, the GAO calculated how much was actually spent in contrast to how much the CBO budgeted or predicted in 1965. Congress and the CBO underestimated the cost of Medicare by 854 percent. (*See* CBO.)

Gobeille v. Liberty Mutual: See SCOTUS.

Guaranteed issue = a rule that requires insurance carriers to accept any patient for coverage, regardless of any pre-existing health condition the patient might have and, thus, regardless of how much that individual might cost the insurance plan.

"Healthcare is a sick patient." = This is my way of saying that only a medical approach can fix our dysfunctional healthcare system. Political and financial approaches over the past 50 years have made the patient called "Healthcare" sicker, not healthier.

Health Insurance Exchange (HIE) = a major component of PPAHCA, where people can shop for health insurance, and those who qualify, which is 70 percent of the U.S. population, can obtain subsidies to reduce out-of-pocket costs. Eighteen states are operating their own exchanges. The majority have decided not to create state-based exchanges: their citizens must obtain insurance through the FFM at www.healthcare.gov. (*See* FFM.)

High-risk pool = refers to those Americans with expensive, usually chronic medical conditions whose annual medical expenses make it difficult-to-impossible to obtain health insurance.

HIPAA = <u>H</u>ealth <u>I</u>nsurance <u>P</u>ortability and <u>A</u>ccountability <u>A</u>ct of 1996. Intended to solve the problem of losing health insurance when losing a job—it did nothing to fix this. HIPAA created a massive regulatory machine, a host of burdensome rules, and tens of billions of dollars in costs, all supposedly to protect the confidentiality of medical information—and it doesn't.

HITECH = <u>H</u>ealth <u>I</u>nformation <u>T</u>echnology for <u>E</u>conomic and <u>C</u>linical <u>H</u>ealth Act. This was part of the American Recovery and Reinvestment Act of 2009. It was intended to create medical information technology standards and infrastructure, and to strengthen the security of personal health information.

Hobby Lobby decision = See SCOTUS: *Burwell v. Hobby Lobby*.

HSA = <u>H</u>ealth <u>S</u>avings <u>A</u>ccount. A bank account owned by an individual in which contributions are not subject to federal taxes. The funds can roll over through the years and accumulate. They can be used only for approved medical expenses. Obamacare limits the amount you can withdraw from an HSA.

ICD-10 = <u>I</u>nternational <u>C</u>lassification of <u>D</u>iseases. A complex, almost incomprehensible billing and coding system that doctors, pharmacists, therapists, and hospitals are required to use if they want to be paid. In addition to illness and injuries, ICD codebooks also include procedures, devices, and anything else that has to do with paying for health care goods and services.

IHS = **I**ndian **H**ealth **S**ervice is a federal agency within the Department of Health and Human Services to provide health services to approximately 2.2 million American Indians and Alaska Natives. IHS is not an entitlement (enrollees pay); is not an insurance plan (it contracts with numerous insurers); and does not have a mandated benefits package like the ACA.

Incentive = a motivator that either encourages someone to perform some behavior (colloquially called a "carrot," or reward) or discourages someone from doing something (a "stick," or punishment). Low prices, for insurance, are a positive incentive to purchase. PPAHCA's tax penalty for not buying insurance is a negative incentive, or "stick."

Individual mandate = the cornerstone of PPAHCA: a federal mandate or requirement that each citizen (does not apply to noncitizens or undocumented immigrants) purchase health insurance. This was struck down by the Supreme Court, which then said it would be constitutional if it were called a "tax." It is the first time American citizens can be "taxed" (penalized) if they *don't* buy something, in this case, health insurance.

Insurance principle = principle by which small contributions of the many pay the great (large) expenses of the few. Lots of people put small amounts of money into a common "risk pool," and a small number of people take out large amounts of money.

IPAB = **I**ndependent **P**ayment **A**dvisory **B**oard. Created by the ACA, this federal agency is tasked with reducing healthcare spending. It is imperative that you read more about this secretive committee, as it will directly impact what care you can receive and what may be denied to you.

IPAB was recently renamed HTAC (Health Technology Assessment Committee). IPAB was what former Governor Sarah Palin famously called a "Death Panel" in 2009. Read more about this in *The Cancer in the American Healthcare System*.

"It just stands to reason." = a phrase used by those who have no hard evidence to support their position or plan. They rely on appeal to emotion.

Job lock = being stuck in a job you do not want to do because you will lose your insurance benefits if you leave. In February, 2014, the CBO released a report predicting that PPAHCA would cause the loss of more than two million jobs in the United States. Nancy Pelosi (D-CA, 12th District), a strong proponent of the ACA and former majority leader of the House of Representatives, hailed this result, saying that Americans would no longer "be job locked but can [as a result of PPAHCA] follow their passion," meaning they could work at what they chose, or decide not to work at all.

King v. Burwell: See SCOTUS.

Learn = to acquire data, knowledge, understanding, and (hopefully) wisdom. To learn requires you to question what you have been taught is true, and sometimes to unlearn that so you can learn what *is* true. As I have written, "Today's 'best medical practice' can be tomorrow's malpractice."

Little Sisters of the Poor v. Burwell: See SCOTUS: *Zubrik v.Burwell*.

MACRA = <u>M</u>edicare <u>A</u>ccess and <u>C</u>HIP <u>R</u>eauthorization <u>A</u>ct of 2015; this act changed how doctors are paid by the two named federal programs. **Market-based medicine** = a healthcare system where medical and financial decisions are decentralized and made by millions of consumers; where there is no federal control of healthcare; where there is no third-party decision maker; and where insurance returns to its original function.

Market failure = when the free market—where consumers spend their own money and prices can vary—does not allocate goods and services *efficiently*, giving the best and cheapest stuff to the most people. The usual alternative suggested to a free market is central (government) control, which has been shown over and over to be *inefficient*—giving the most to a small number of elite people and little-to-nothing to the public at large. This is not conservative bias. It is based on the hard evidence of history.

Medicaid = an *entitlement* program, in contrast to Medicare. You qualify by low income, age, or having certain chronic conditions. You pay nothing and receive benefits dictated by the government. (Contrast to Medicare.)

Medical malpractice (tort) system = a system that supposedly punishes the wrongdoer and compensates the injured when a patient is injured or harmed in relation to medical care. An alternative system called the Office of Medical Injuries is proposed in my forthcoming e-book *We Need Tort Replacement, Not Reform*.

Medicare (contrast to Medicaid) = a program (but *not* an entitlement program) conceived as a giant Health Savings Account (HSA), where you put in money for 40 years. You paid into it during your whole working career. When you retired, that very large pot of money, which accumulated and grew, would pay all the medical expenses of your golden years. Read in *The Cancer in the American Healthcare System* how and why Congress subverted Medicare.

MERP = <u>M</u>edicaid <u>E</u>state <u>R</u>ecovery <u>P</u>rogram. Passed as part of the Omnibus Budget Recovery Act of 1993, this law allows state governments to recoup a $611-per-month administrative fee (which could total as much as $73,310) and property after the death of a Medicaid recipient. To this, the states can add a bill for 10 to 40 percent of a patient's total medical bills that were paid through Medicaid.

Metal level = percent of your health care costs that are covered by insurance plans that are ACA-compliant. Using the names of metals signifies different levels: Bronze (60 percent of your costs are covered); Silver (70 percent); Gold (80 percent); and Platinum (90 percent). Of course, the cost of the insurance premium goes up considerably, depending on which "metal" level you choose: Bronze = cheapest; Platinum = most costly. As the cost rises, the benefits also increase.

Micro-economic disconnection = the separation of the consumer from control of his or her own money. This makes it impossible for the free market to function, as supply and demand can no longer balance each other.

Moral hazard = refers to the danger to society of some people spending other people's money and therefore having no need to economize or to act responsibly or morally.

Navigator = a person available to help individuals through the complexity of purchasing health insurance. PPAHCA requires each state to have them. These individuals are presumably impartial, or not paid by or beholden to any insurance carrier, as brokers can be. Navigators are also called "in-person assisters."

Net (when calculating pretty much anything) = a word I frequently use because too many people look exclusively at the short-term cost, without considering long-term costs and without evaluating benefits at all. A "net calculation" for spending on healthcare would determine *value*—what we *really* care about—by comparing long-term costs and risks to long-term benefits to patients.

NFIB v. Sebelius: See SCOTUS.

NHS = <u>N</u>ational <u>H</u>ealth <u>S</u>ervice. This is the name of the government-run healthcare system in Great Britain. It was used as a model for the original version of Obamacare.

NICE = <u>N</u>ational <u>I</u>nstitute for <u>C</u>linical <u>E</u>xcellence. A component of the NHS that was the model for the IPAB that is part of Obamacare. Both NICE and IPAB are tasked with cost cutting by deciding what medical care will be authorized and therefore available for use in patients. These groups also decide what types of care will be denied, or deemed not cost effective, even if the treatment works medically.

Payer = a term that can be confusing. In most aspects of your life, the payer *is* the *consumer*; they are one and the same. In a free market, the consumer/payer gives money to the supplier in exchange for goods and services. Healthcare, with its third-party payer system, is not a free market. The consumer does not directly pay the supplier and therefore is not the payer. The *supplier* (provider) does not set his or her price. The government, not the market, determines the price. There is a third-party *payer* who either has no incentive to economize (the government) or is rewarded, or incentivized, when it denies payment for care (insurance).

PBM = <u>P</u>harmacy <u>B</u>enefits <u>M</u>anager. This is a computer program implemented by many health plans that doctors must use to order medications. The program tells the doctor what drugs he or she can or cannot use (usually determined by cost, not medical efficacy for that patient). If the doctor wants to use a nonapproved drug, there is a complex, time-consuming process to appeal the health plan's restriction.

PCIP = <u>P</u>re-Existing <u>C</u>ondition <u>I</u>nsurance <u>P</u>rogram. A component of the Affordable Care Act that was supposed to provide insurance for those usually *uninsurable* because of expensive pre-existing medical conditions. Enrollment was discontinued after less than a third of the eligible people signed up. The chairman of the New Mexico High Risk Insurance Pool said, "Washington just left the sickest of Americans high and dry, holding nothing but an empty promise."

Perverse incentive = a system that rewards someone when they do the opposite of what is wanted. In retail, this would be giving a bonus to the person who sells the fewest products. Incentives in healthcare are perverse when insurance is rewarded (makes profit) by delaying, deferring, or denying medical care you need now! In chapter 3 of my ebook *Our Allies Have Become Our Enemies* I call this the Strategy of the Three D's.

Phantom code = a billing code used by a health care provider to charge for a service he or she did not actually provide. This is fraud.

PNHP = <u>P</u>hysicians for a <u>N</u>ational <u>H</u>ealth <u>P</u>rogram. A political activist group that advocates for a single payer approach for the United States. Their position is discussed in *Single Payer Won't Save Us*.

Population medicine = doing what is medically best, as decided by some panel of experts (self-styled), for the population as a whole. That means the needs of the group supersede the needs of the individual. Doctors are ethically committed to the opposite: *personal* medicine.

Primum non nocere = Latin phrase considered the *prime directive* for physicians and is commonly but incorrectly translated as "First (above all), do no harm." A more precise interpretation of the original Latin yields, "At least, do no harm!"

Provider (of health care) = anyone whose activities *directly* affect a patient, such as a doctor, nurse, respiratory therapist, or social worker. Many others, not called providers, *indirectly* affect patient welfare, such as billers, coders, managers, legislators, regulators, support staff, or technicians.

Psychic reward = an emotional or psychological, nonmaterial payment for a service, product, or action. For most health care providers, the psychic reward for helping others is more important than the monetary reward.

Public option = is a shorthand colloquial term for single payer, in contrast to having multiple entities, usually insurance carriers, but sometimes health organizations, who pay the costs for health care goods and services. Many use the Canadian system as an example of a public option.

Ration = to "make reasonable," or to apply logic and reason to a problem. In Economics, to *ration* is "to balance supply and demand."

Regulatory burden = a mountain of federal regulations that control every aspect of healthcare, from the financing to the day-to-day practice of medicine. The cost of compliance with these regulations is massive in money, provider frustration, medical errors, and time taken away from patient care *by federal mandate*. The dollar cost of the federal regulatory bureaucracy is now more than 40 percent of *all* U.S. healthcare spending.

Rent-seeking behavior = behavior by a private company seeking to obtain economic advantage through government intervention, such as tariff protection or cost-sharing reductions ("bailouts"). By definition, the economic gain does not produce any benefit to society through wealth creation. Rent-seeking is government redistribution to benefit a favored commercial enterprise.

Rescission = insurance industry jargon for canceling an insurance policy, sometimes for frivolous reasons or with a trumped-up excuse.

Right (to health care) = being entitled to health care (the service) when you want, where you want, what you want, for free, without needing to qualify in any way. Proponents say that by simply being alive, you have this right. The relationship between a right to health care and one's personal responsibility has never been openly discussed. I believe the lack of consensus on this matter is at the heart of problems in our healthcare system.

Romneycare = colloquial term for the Massachusetts health care insurance reform act signed into law in April 2006, while Mitt Romney was governor. The proper name for this system is Commonwealth Care. There are many similarities between Romneycare and Obamacare, but they are not identical.

Root cause ("etiology" is the medical term) = the primary, or first, cause. This is the "why" of illness. In diabetes, the symptoms are related to elevated sugar in the blood, but elevated sugar is not the root cause, which is due to failure of insulin to regulate blood sugar. Dysfunction or improper production of insulin is the root cause in diabetes. Has anyone shown you the root causes to explain why our healthcare system is "broken"?

SCOTUS = **S**upreme **C**ourt **of** **t**he **U**nited **S**tates. The five major ACA-related cases that have been heard by the Supreme Court are listed below:

1. **2012:** *NFIB v. Sebelius* = The National Federation of Independent Business sued then-Secretary of Health and Human Services, Kathleen Sebelius, challenging both the individual mandate and the mandatory expansion of all state Medicaid programs. SCOTUS struck down both as unconstitutional. Then, in this 5–4 decision, they said the federal government could keep the individual mandate if they changed the name to a "tax." Medicaid expansion remained voluntary.

2. **2014:** *Burwell v. Hobby Lobby* = Obamacare requires all insurance to provide 10 essential benefits, which include contraceptives and abortifacients (agents/drugs that induce abortion). Christian-based Hobby Lobby Company sued, claiming that the ACA violated their right to religious freedom (First Amendment). After years of lower-court hearings, the Supreme Court heard the case, agreed with Hobby Lobby, and prohibited the federal government from penalizing religious-based organizations for failure to offer contraceptives and abortifacients.

3. **2015:** *King v. Burwell* = David King and three other plaintiffs sued Sylvia Burwell as Secretary of Health and Human Ser-

vices. They claimed that the federal government was illegally providing subsidies because healthcare.gov is an exchange created by the *federal* government, but the ACA says subsidies can be provided only through exchanges "established by the *state*." The IRS issued a ruling that healthcare.gov could provide subsidies even though the ACA said it could not. In a 6–3 decision, SCOTUS upheld the IRS, opining they understood that Congress wanted to give subsidies to everyone, even if the law wasn't written that way.

4. **2016:** *Gobeille v. Liberty Mutual* = Vermont wanted to create a statewide database for healthcare. When they sought to require carriers to provide their information, Liberty Mutual refused, claiming federal law—ERISA, the Employee Retirement Income Security Act of 1974—prevented them from complying. The Supreme Court decided in Liberty Mutual's favor, that federal law superseded state law. The decision will reduce the amount of data available to consumers of care services.

5. **2016:** *Zubrik v. Burwell* = The Hobby Lobby decision (above) was written with very narrow applicability. Therefore, Obamacare was still allowed to use healthcare dollars to support, albeit indirectly, abortion, contraception, and "birth preventative services." A number of Catholic organizations, led by the Little Sisters of the Poor, sued the federal government, claiming Obamacare violated their right to religious freedom (First Amendment). During oral arguments in April 2016, the justices took the unusual step of asking the litigants if they could settle their differences without a Court decision. The Little Sisters said yes, but the government said no. The Supreme Court then decided . . . not to decide. Their unanimous, unsigned *decision* was to refer the case back to lower courts to find a compromise without holding either for plaintiff or defendant.

6. **2018:** *Texas et al. v. U.S.A.* = A coalition of states led by Texas sued in circuit court to repeal the ACA. Their rationale was

as follows: In *NFIB v. Sebelius*, the federal government argued strongly that the entire act was dependent on the individual mandate and was unsustainable without it. SCOTUS declared the mandate unconstitutional but said that it could survive if structured as a tax.

The Tax Cuts and Jobs Act of 2017 reduced the ACA individual mandate tax to zero, thus eliminating it. Based on the logic and facts above, the Northern District of Texas Circuit Court struck down the ACA but put a stay on implementation of the repeal, pending the inevitable appeals. This case will no doubt be decided by the Supreme Court, probably in 2020 or 2021.

SHOP = **S**mall Business **H**ealth **O**ptions **P**rogram. This is a part of the ACA that offers insurance plans to small businesses.

Signup (enrollee) = as counted by Washington, anyone who has completed the application process for insurance, even if that person is not covered, no card is issued, and/or the person has never paid a premium.

Single Payer system = where the government is the distribution source for payments to providers, institutions, suppliers, and (if insurance is used), insurance middlemen. Because it controls both the money and the regulations, the government dictates how much it will pay, what it will pay for, and when. There are no market forces in a single payer system such as those in a free market. Instead, a monopoly (government) controls both supply and demand. The U.S. Veterans Administration is a single payer system, as is the British National Health Service. (*See* public option.)

Spending (noun) = money paid. All too often, "spending" is mistakenly used to mean the same as "cost," which is very different. (*See* cost.)

StatesCare = removing federal control of healthcare and allowing the people in their states to decide what healthcare structure they will have.

Subsidy from ACA. See APTC.

System = a set of connected things or parts that form a complex structure. The key is the word "connected," because without the structure and minus the connections, parts are just a pile of stuff that can do nothing.

Systems thinking = a management approach that emphasizes the need to study the intact system or entire structure as a whole. When you break it up and study each part separately, you lose the connections and its "system-ness." Practicing good medicine on anyone requires systems thinking. A good doctor would never do something to improve kidney function without considering how that treatment might affect other organs such as the heart, lungs, or liver.

TANSTAAFL = "There Ain't No Such Thing As A Free Lunch." It means that nothing in this world is free, nothing. *Someone* has to pay for it, whatever "it" is.

The Three D's = a strategy used by health care payers to hold on to your money as long as possible: delay, defer, or deny.

"Trust me! I have your best interests at heart." = This is a common catchphrase of those who take a paternalistic attitude toward others and control them, for their own good, of course!

Two-master dilemma = the problem of who should be your first priority: your employer or your customer; your patient's best interests or following regulations. I call this the "who-master dilemma."

UMRA = Unfunded Mandates Reform Act of 1995. This act was intended to fix the problem created by EMTALA, which created the unfunded mandate: the law that requires hospitals to treat patients for free, which in turn makes them overcharge paying patients to avoid bankruptcy. UMRA did not resolve the unfunded mandate, which is now an even bigger problem than it was in 1995. (*See* EMTALA.)

Uncompensated care = medical care that a hospital must provide by law for which it receives no payment—the unfunded mandate. This was an unintended consequence of EMTALA (*See* EMTALA.)

Underinsured = The purpose of insurance is to prevent financial disaster in the event of an expensive medical catastrophe. As many as 84 million Americans have medical insurance in which the coverage is too low to protect them from medical bankruptcy. These are the *"under*insured."

Unfunded mandate. *See* EMTALA; also uncompensated care.

Uninsured = those who have no medical insurance. Current estimates put this number at 45 to 50 million Americans, 24 percent of whom are not legal citizens. Because of EMTALA, sick patients can always get care whether they have insurance or not, and it is paid for by someone else—in most cases, the U.S. taxpayer.

Universal health care = national healthcare systems in which reputedly everyone gets care. I write "reputedly" because these systems are not *universal* (noncitizens do not get free care). *Care may be denied* by government decree and often is. For example, there is Canada, where people sometimes cannot get the care they need when they need it.

Up-code = when a provider submits a billing code for a higher-paying service than actually provided, thus generating a higher charge. In the extreme, the doctor removes tonsils and codes the bill for open-heart surgery.

"We the Patients" = We the Patients emphasizes our commonality—every person is now a patient or eventually will be a patient. We the Patients includes Democrats and Republicans, rich and poor, all ages and stages, and American citizens as well as people here illegally. If you are alive in the United States, you are part of We the Patients. We are all in "this" together, where "this" means life in the United States.

Index

About the Author

Why should you read what Dr. Deane writes? Because he is your "go to" guy if you want to understand your healthcare system and, more important, know what to do about it. With both an MD and MBA, Dr. Deane is your most credible source for five reasons:

1. He received his education and training at Yale, Chicago Med, the Mayo Clinic, Northwestern, Harvard, and Anderson Management School;

2. He is former director of the Center for Health Care Policy at the Texas Public Policy Foundation based in Austin, Texas;

3. During almost 40 years as a pediatric cardiologist, he has experienced every aspect of healthcare, including being a patient himself in an ICU, twice;

4. Dr. Deane is able to make our healthcare system understandable to the average person; and

5. He has no political agenda. Dr. Deane simply wants to treat a sick system we call patient healthcare using the principles of good medical practice.

Dr. Deane is a widely recognized authority, both speaking as well as writing articles and books. He has published more than 150 academic medical articles and monographs along with more than 300 articles for the general public about healthcare. He has been published in *Huffington Post*, *Fox News*, *American Thinker*, *Op-Ed News*, *The Blaze*, *Forbes*, *The Hill*, *Real Clear Health*, *The Federalist*, *Investor's Business Daily*, and the *Washington Examiner*, as well as newspapers including *USA Today*, *Houston Chronicle*, and the *Wall Street Journal*. Dr. Deane is interviewed frequently on broadcast radio and podcasts.

Dr. Deane has published six print books, titled *Uproot U.S. Healthcare* (now in its second edition); *Cambio Radical al Sistema de Salud de los Estados Unidos* (Spanish translation of the *Uproot* book); multiple-award-winner *The Cancer in Healthcare*; award- winning *The Cancer in the American Healthcare System*; and now his culminating work, *Curing the Cancer in U.S. Healthcare*. He has released six of the seven e-books in the best-selling series *Restoring Care to American Healthcare*.

Outside of medicine, Dr. Deane has had some . . . *interesting* life experiences. As a child, he was in the Middle East when the 1956 war broke out. He was an exchange student in Berlin in 1961 when the Wall went up between East and West Germany. Thirty-seven years later, in 1998, Dr. Deane had the pleasure of revisiting Berlin with the Wall gone and the city reunited. In 1968, Dr. Deane patched up the injured during the Democratic National Convention in Chicago, and in 2013, he acted as "war correspondent," writing articles for *The Blaze* from Istanbul during the Silent Revolution. Dr. Deane says his life priorities are as follows: his family, We the Patients, and bicycle racing on the track (velodrome), in that order.

Would you review this book?

If you loved this book, would you please
provide a review at Amazon.com?

CPSIA information can be obtained
at www.ICGtesting.com
Printed in the USA
LVHW050850291019
635546LV00003B/958/P